The media's taken notice of Va
sampling of our coverage.

"Vault is vastly popular...a cyber success."
– *NPR Marketplace*

"Each report is packed with nuggets on pay, perks and promotion policies, as well as typical curveball interview questions and the dirt on company culture, written in an edgy, no-holds-barred style."
– *P.O.V Magazine*

"Boasting a cutting-edge filtering technology, Vault.com says it's found the solution to the tight job recruiting market."
– *USA Today*

"Another killer app for the Internet."
–*New York Times*

"Vault gives you a lot of insight that you might not find anywhere else. It makes homework a lot more fun than it was in fifth grade."
–*San Francisco Examiner*

"The site's big attractions are the lively and candid company profiles. These sometimes biting commentaries touch on everything from salaries to dress codes to office atmosphere."
– *Publisher's Weekly*

Four Stars – "Best way to research potential employers."
–*Yahoo! Internet Life*

VAULT.COM GUIDE TO FINANCE INTERVIEWS

Vault.com Guide to Finance Interviews

D. BHATAWEDEKHAR AND THE STAFF OF VAULT.COM

Copyright © 1999 by Vault, Inc. All rights reserved.

All information in this book is subject to change without notice. Vault.com makes no claims as to the accuracy and reliability of the information contained within and disclaims all warranties. No part of this book may be reproduced or transmitted in any form or by any means, electronic or mechanical, for any purpose, without the express written permission of Vault, Inc.

Vault.com, and the Open Vault logo are trademarks of Vault, Inc.

For information about permission to reproduce selections from this book, contact Vault Reports Inc., P.O. Box 1772, New York, New York 10011-1772, (212) 366-4212.

Library of Congress CIP Data is available.

ISBN 1-58131-101-X

Printed in the United States of America

ACKNOWLEDGEMENTS

Vault.com would like to thank:

Mark Hernandez, Glenn Fischer, Carole and Bart Fischer, Lee Black, Ed Somekh, Todd Kelleher, Bruce Bland, Gary Mueller, Ravi Mhatre, Tom Phillips, Ken Cron, Alison Harmelin, J. Shelby Bryan, Jan Brzeski, Chris & Bob Burch, Bob Cymbala, Celeste and Noelle, Muriel and Stephanie, Michael Kalt, Bryan Finkel, Jay Oyakawa, Geoff Baum, Brian Fischer, Glen and Dorothy Wilkins, Sarah Griffith, C.J. Nilsson, Geoff Vitale, Dana Evans, and our families.

And to:

Miguel Abreu, Faisal Anwar, Alex Apelbaum, Alan Audi, Robert Birgfeld, Gery Blumenthal, Lee Borom, Doug Cantor, Chris Casso, Archana Chand, Ada Chu, Karson Clancy, Christine Clayton, Clifford Cook, Christine Curtis, Laurie Duncan, Al Gatling, Danilo Gavilanes, Andrew Gillies, Emily Gold, Neil Goldstein, Kathryn Goyne, Nadine Grasso, Jon Green, Alexis Green, Sharay Harris, Stephanie Hartman, Wendy Herzberg, Jeff Holden, Brent Johnson, Kate Kaibni, Chris Knepler, Sylvia Kovac, Todd Kuhlman, Peter Latshaw, Michael Lee, Marcy Lerner, Shirley Lin, Sherry Lin, Clarissa Londis, Eduardo Lopez, Joan Lucas, Justin Martin, Ja' Moore, Corrie Moore, Candice Mortimer, David Moss, Keith Nagel, Thomas Nutt, Jessica O'Brien, Brenda Ortiz, Vassili Petrov, Jordan Pflugh, Candace Popkin, Chandra Prasad, Maribelle Ramos, Andrew Reale, Kevin Salgado, Matthew Samet, Robert Schipano, Rose Schipano, Nikki Scott, Peter Serwe, Jamil Shamasdin, Austin Shau, Ed Shen, Ewa Smieszek, Daniel Sanco, Carolyn Stein, Boby Suriyathep, Angela Tong, Sohrab Torabi, Pablo Usandivaras, Nakia Vernon, Jake Wallace, Kamil Wigla, Kedda Williams, Karina Williams, and last but not least, Noah Zucker.

CONTENTS

Introduction   1

    The finance interview: An overview 4

    Questions 9

Valuation Techniques   15

    Basic accounting concepts 16

    Market valuation 22

    Discounted cash flow analysis (DCF) 23

    Comparable transactions 37

    Multiples 38

    Questions 40

Stocks   53

    A remedial lesson 53

    Equity vs. debt 53

    Preferred stock 54

    Dividends 55

    Stock splits 55

    Stock buybacks 55

    New stock issues 56

    Questions 57

Bonds & Interest Rates   63

    What is a bond? A remedial lesson 63

    Bond terminology 63

    How a bond works 64

    Pricing bonds 65

CONTENTS

Other bond concepts 66
The Fed and interest rates 67
The Fed and inflation 68
Effect of inflation on bond prices 69
Leading Economic indicators 70
Questions 71

Currencies   77

Exchange rates 77
Influence of interest rates on foreign exchange 78
Influence of inflation on foreign exchange 78
Capital market equilibrium 79
The three factors 80
Effect of exchange rates on earnings of companies 80
Effect of exchange rates on interest rates and inflation 80
Currency devaluation and revaluation 81
Questions 82

Options & Derivatives   85

Options 86
Writing options 86
Summary options chart 87
Options pricing 87
Forwards, futures, and swaps 89
Questions 91

CONTENTS

Mergers & Acquisitions — 95

- Why merger? 95
- Why not merge? 96
- Stock swaps vs. cash offers 96
- Tender offers 97
- Mergers vs. acquisitions 98
- We love pooling accounting 98
- Will that be cash or stock? 101
- Accretive vs. dilutive mergers 101
- Questions 103

Brainteasers & Guesstimates — 107

- Acing guesstimates 107
- Brainteasers 108
- Quick: What's 2 + 2? 109
- Questions 110

Final Analysis — 121

Appendix — 123

- Glossary 123

In the 1980s, Greed was Good.
In the Information Age...
GOSSIP IS GOOD

Use our Message Boards to:

- Share in the latest company gossip
- Get the inside scoop on pay, perks and bonuses
- Hear about interviews from recent candidates
- Mix and interact with other job seekers
- Post messages and start your own discussions

Come see what they are saying now about the employers on your interview list!

Message boards available on 1000s of top employers, including:

3Com	Cargill	The Gap	Morgan Stanley
A.T. Kearney	Citibank/Citigroup	General Mills	Netscape Comunications
Abbott Laboratories	Clorox	Goldman, Sachs & Co	Nike
America Online	Coca-Cola	Hewlett-Packard	Oracle
American Express	Colgate-Palmolive	IBM	Procter & Gamble
AMS	Credit Suisse First Boston	Intel	PricewaterhouseCoopers
Andersen Consulting	Dell Computer	Johnson & Johnson	Salomon Smith Barney
Arthur D. Little	Deloitte Consulting	J.P. Morgan	Silicon Graphics
Aveda	DLJ	KPMG Consulting	Sprint
Bain	Enron	Levi Strauss	Sun Microsystems
Bankers Trust	Ernst & Young	Merck	Time Warner
Boston Consulting Group	Fidelity	Microsoft	Walt Disney
Booz-Allen & Hamilton	Ford Motor Company	Mobil	

W W W . V A U L T . C O M

Get the Inside Scoop

with Vault.com 50- to 70-page Premium Employer Profiles

Vault.com Premium Employer Profiles are FREE 50- to 70-page reports on leading employers. These profiles give you the straight story on recent developments, company culture, pay, interviews, hiring practices, and more at top companies and firms. Based on our research and exclusive insider interviews of 1,000s of employees, these reports are available online at Vault.com

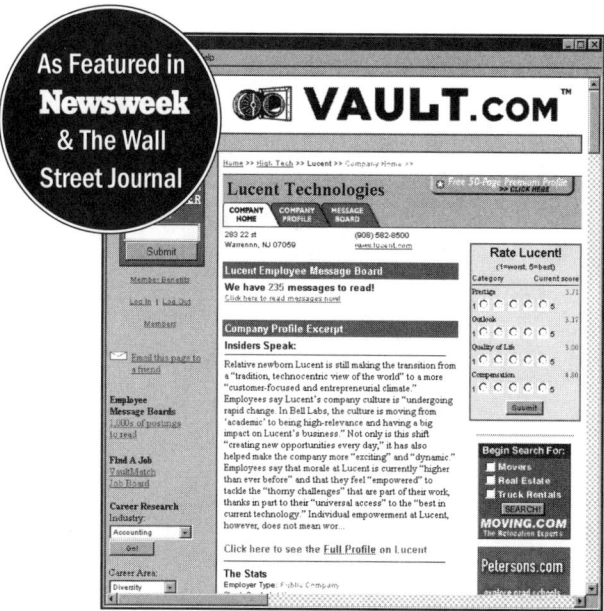

As Featured in **Newsweek** & The Wall Street Journal

FREE online at

VAULT.COM

Premium Employer Profiles

American Express	General Mills
American Management Systems	Goldman Sachs
Andersen Consulting	Hewlett-Packard
Arthur Andersen	Intel
Arthur D. Little	JP Morgan
AT Kearney	KPMG
Bain & Co.	Lehman Brothers
Bear Stearns	McKinsey & Co.
Booz Allen & Hamilton	Mercer Management Consulting
Boston Consulting Group	Merrill Lynch
Cargill	Microsoft
Citicorp/Citibank	Mitchell Madison Group
Coca-Cola	Monitor Company
Credit Suisse First Boston	Morgan Stanley Dean Witter
Deloitte & Touche	Oracle
Donaldson Lufkin & Jenrette	PricewaterhouseCoopers
Enron	Procter & Gamble
Ernst & Young	Salomon Smith Barney
Fidelity Investments	Sprint
Ford Motor	Walt Disney
Gemini	

.......many more!

"Fun read, edgy details" — *Forbes*

"Each report is packed with nuggets on pay, perks and promotion policies, as well as typical curveball interview questions and the dirt on company culture, written in an edgy, no-holds-barred style."
— *P.O.V. magazine*

Four Stars - "Best way to research potential employers" — *Yahoo! Internet Life*

Read our Premium Employer Profiles for FREE at www.Vault.com

Introduction

Money makes the world go round, and those in charge of the money are the financiers. Have a thirst for relevance?

Finance career opportunities can be broadly divided into several categories, most prominently investment banking, commercial banking, asset management, venture capital and private equity, and finance positions at a corporation like Dell or The Coca-Cola Company (also called "finance in a company"). There is considerable movement between these positions — I-bankers leave to take posts in industry, or with private equity firms, etc. Generally, the pinnacle for most finance professionals is either as a partner or managing director of a bank, a portfolio manager for an asset management firm, or as Chief Financial Officer (CFO) of a company. Let's take a brief look at some of the major industries for finance positions.

Investment banking

Tom Wolfe called them "Masters of the Universe" in *The Bonfire of the Vanities*; Michael Lewis called them a few unprintable things in *Liar's Poker*. Who are they? Investment bankers, salespeople, traders, and research analysts. Investment banks aren't like your local branch office with ubiquitous ATMs (those are commercial banks, like Citibank or Bank of America); instead, investment banks work with corporations, governments, institutional investors and extraordinarily wealthy individuals to raise capital and provide investment advice.

However, the legal barrier between commercial and investment banks has been rapidly decaying since the 1980s, and this decade has witnessed the arrival of huge commercial banks entering the investment banking market. Commercial banks have been acquiring small-to medium-sized investment banks at a rapid rate. Baltimore-based Alex. Brown, the oldest investment bank in the nation, was recently acquired by Bankers Trust (Bankers Trust itself was bought by German titan Deutsche Bank) and commercial titan Bank of America snapped up fast-growing Robertson Stephens only to sell it to BankBoston after merging with another major commercial bank, NationsBank. (NationsBank had acquired its own investment bank, Montgomery Securities.)

Mergers between investment banks and retail brokerage houses are another trend — witness the recent conjoinings of Morgan Stanley and Dean Witter, Discover, and Salomon Brothers and Smith Barney (now called Salomon Smith Barney). Furthermore, these investment banks are also combining with commercial banks (for example, Salomon Smith Barney's parent company, Travelers, merged with commercial banking giant Citicorp to form Citigroup). These combinations and mergers mean big changes and big opportunities in the investment banking industry. Despite the turmoil, positions in these temples of lucre remain highly sought after.

Commercial banking

Generally, commercial banks are "lenders" rather than "bankers." In other words, they loan money rather than raise it. You can go to the local branch office of your bank and apply for a loan, but you can't ask them to find investors to fund your latest get-rich-quick scheme. Similarly, commercial banks will loan out large amounts of money to businesses (sometimes banding together with other banks for especially huge loans to issue what is called a "syndicated loan"), but traditionally, could not raise money for clients by bringing stock offerings to the public. Commercial banks lend out money at interest rates that are largely determined by the Federal Reserve Board (currently governed by the bespectacled Alan Greenspan). The Fed loans out money to commercial banks, which turns around and lends it to its customers in a variety of forms — standard loans, mortgages, etc. Commercial banks also lend out money that they have on deposit from clients. (For a more detailed description of how the Fed operates, refer to the chapter on bonds and interest rates.)

These days, the legal wall between commercial banking and investment banking, which was erected in the aftermath of the Depression, is being torn down. Many commercial banks are buying investment banking arms, adding I-banking capabilities, or in some cases, like J.P. Morgan and Chase Manhattan, transforming themselves into investment banks, providing money-raising capabilities to clients with whom they had previously had lending relationships. Commercial bankers and investment bankers are notoriously different culturally: commercial bankers are typically less aggressive and more risk-averse than investment bankers. They also don't command the eye-popping bonuses that I-bankers can receive. As more commercial banks become driven by investment banking businesses, culture clash will be an important factor in whether these combinations work.

Investment management

The investment management industry, or, as it's also known, asset management, can be broken down into three basic categories: hedge funds and proprietary trading desks, mutual funds and the asset management divisions of investment banks, and 'other' — which includes insurance companies, universities, municipal governments, and other large institutions with money to invest. Asset managers are the "customers," or "buy-side" of an institutional sale of financial securities. On the "sell-side" are the traders and salespeople, who provide liquidity for the asset managers.

The name of the industry, investment management, is pretty much self-explanatory: a client gives money to an asset manager or fund manager, who then invests it to meet the client's objectives. The people on the sell-side provide information to the buy-side (research, ideas, meetings with officials), and try to get the asset managers to trade through them (the sell-side makes a commission for every trade it facilitates). These days, many banks are looking to grow their asset management business because they are largely protected against the volatility of the market. Asset managers are generally paid a percentage of the entire amount they handle, whether they make or lose money for the client. Because their salaries are based on the amount of money they manage, asset managers make less money than investment bankers (unless they work for hedge funds). They don't necessarily make big bonuses, but on the upside, they know what they're getting paid whether they make or lose money for the client. Be advised, however, that asset managers typically have contract terms of three years or less — AMs can't keep clients if they underperform.

Venture capital

Venture capital (VC), says one insider, is the R&D of the 1990s. For the past six years, venture capital firms have been on a roll — and the cream of the crop of MBA programs across the country are clawing for a spot in these tiny, highly profitable enterprises. Landing a VC job requires smarts, a thorough understanding of business operations (so one can tell how a company is operating and where it can improve), but perhaps most of all, great connections.

Venture capital companies typically invest between $250,000 and $20 million in seed to private companies in exchange for equity — a piece of the firm. Venture firms raise their money from pension funds, endowments, corporations, and wealthy individuals. Venture capitalists are in it for the money — and with the Internet boom, that can be quite a bit of money indeed. Imagine the profits enjoyed by Sequoia Capital, which took a 20 percent stake in Yahoo! for a mere $1 million. The stake was worth billions in less than five years.

Industry

Finance officials with corporations can perform a wide variety of functions, which range from managing a company's stock buyback strategy, to internal auditing, to cost, pricing or profitability analysis. In some cases, these positions can be similar to investment banking positions. For example, many large companies maintain small internal M&A arms, which seek out acquisition opportunities, and help structure those deals. Companies with large international operations also often employ financial whizzes to help them hedge their foreign exchange risk.

The entry-level position in the finance function at corporations is usually called "financial analyst." The peak is the chief financial officer (CFO) position. Throughout a finance career in industry, employees work closely with other functions (most commonly marketing and operations), partly to report and explain financial statements, and partly to hash out both short-term and long-term strategy.

The basics

While the requirements of each of these industries vary somewhat, the basic concepts for interviews for finance positions are the same:

- Know the industry you are looking to get into
- Research the company
- Meet with people who work at the company
- Understand the job you will be doing well
- Have some good questions ready that you may want to ask

The Finance Interview: An Overview

Investment banking positions and other finance positions are some of the more stressful and demanding positions on the planet, and the interviews reflect this fact. In fact, insiders say that occasionally, an interviewer will yell at an applicant to see how he or she will react. Interviews normally go three or four rounds (sometimes as many as six or more rounds), and these rounds can have up to six interviews each, especially in the later rounds. Investment banking and finance interviews are also known for being deliberately stressful (as opposed to the attendant nervousness that goes with any interview). Some firms may ask you specific and detailed questions about your grades in college or business school, even if your school policy prohibits such questions. At other firms, interview rounds may be interspersed with seemingly casual and friendly dinners. Don't let down your guard! While these dinners are a good opportunity to meet your prospective co-workers, your seemingly genial hosts are scrutinizing you as well. (Hint: Don't drink too much.)

There are generally two parts to the finance hiring process: the "fit" part, and the technical part. In asking technical questions, the interviewer wants to judge your analytical and technical skills. If you don't know the basic concepts of finance and accounting, your interviewers will believe (rightly) that you are 1) either not interested in the position 2) not competent enough to handle the job. While most of this book will be devoted to helping you ace the technical aspect of finance interviews, arguably a more important part of the interviews is what is called the "fit" interview. As you go through recruiting in finance interviews, understand that you compete with yourself. Most firms are flexible enough to hire people that are a good fit.

The "fit" interview

They call it the O'Hare airport test, the Atlanta airport test, or the whatever-city-you-happen-to-be-applying-in airport test. They also call it the "fit" interview or the "behavioral" interview. It means: "Could you stand to be stranded in an airport for eight hours with this person?" Although bankers may have reputations for being aggressive individuals, don't act that way in your interview.

And while your performance in the fit interview partly depends — as the airport test suggests — on how well you gel with your interviewer, it also depends on your ability to portray yourself as a good "fit" as an investment banker, asset manager, etc. In other words, interviewers will try to suss out what your attitude towards work is like, how interested you are in a career in the industry, and how interested you are in the job for which you are applying particularly.

I'm a hard worker

As a general rule, you should emphasize how hard you have worked in the past, giving evidence of your ability to take on a lot of work and pain. You don't have to make things up or pretend that there's nothing you'd want more than to work 100-hour weeks. In fact, interviewers are sure to see through such blatant lying. Says one

I-banking interviewer, "If somebody acted too enthusiastic about the hours, that'd be weird." If you ask investment bankers and others in finance what they dislike most about their jobs, they will most likely talk about the long hours. Be honest about this unpleasant part of the job, and convince your interviewer that you can handle it well. For example, if you were in crew and had to wake up at five every morning in the freezing cold, by all means, talk about it. And if you put yourself through school by working two jobs, mention that too.

Got safe hands

As with all job interviews, those for finance positions will largely be about figuring out whether you can handle the responsibility required of the position. (In many cases with finance positions, that responsibility will mean making decisions with millions or billions of dollars at stake.)

An interviewer will try and figure out if you've got "safe hands" and won't be dropping the ball. "This is a critical I-banking concept," says one banker about safe hands. The idea is: 'Can I give this person this analysis to do and feel comfortable that they will execute it promptly and correctly?' The people with 'safe hands' are the ones who advance in the company. They are not necessarily the hardest workers but they are the most competent." Make sure you bring up examples of taking responsibility.

A mind to pick things apart

The world of finance is largely about number crunching and analytical ability. While this doesn't mean you have to be a world-class mathematician, it does mean that you have to have an analytic mind if you are to succeed. Explains one insider at a numbers-heavy Wall Street firm, "you can't be any old English major, you've got to have a really logical, mathematical head." Make sure you have examples of your problem-solving and analytic strengths.

T-E-A-M! Go team!

Teamwork is the buzzword of these days not just for the investment banking industry, but for every employer. Every finance position (except, perhaps, for research) requires that an employee work closely with others — whether this be in the form of investment banking deal teams, or finance officials working with marketers at a corporation. Interviewers will ask questions to make sure that you have experience, and have excelled, in team situations. Yeah, you can break out those "glory day" stories about the winning touchdown pass, but lots of other situations can also help describe your teamwork ability — previous work experience, volunteer activities, etc.

Preparing for finance interviews

When you review career options, don't discount the amount of time it takes to prepare for finance interviews. First of all, you should evaluate whether you actually want to be in investment banking, commercial banking, venture capital, etc. In short, you should know what you're getting into. Not only should you know this for your own sake (this is your future, after all), but your interviewers want to know that you understand the position and industry.

You should use the opportunity of "non-evaluative" settings (i.e. not an interview) to get answers to these questions. These are questions to which we strongly suggest you have answers to before interviewing. Make a point to attend recruiting presentations by firms. Your informational interviews with alumni and (for those in business school) second-years are also good ways to get answers to some of your questions.

As for written materials, you can start with Vault.com career guides and other primers for industries. Once you have the basics and the framework down, your best sources are *Investment Dealer's Digest*, *The Wall Street Journal*, *The Economist*, *Business Week*, *Financial Times*, and other business publications.

Your interaction with alumni can have direct results. The results can be good if you prepare properly before contacting them. You can also assure yourself a ding if you don't handle a meeting or phone conversation correctly.

Here are some questions about finance positions you should ask before you have your first interview:

- What is a typical day like?

- What are the hours in the industry really like? Are they 100 hours every week or every other week? Is it the same for every firm?

- How do people cope with the lifestyle issues in the industry?

- What kind of money do people make in the industry?

- What are the things I-bankers (or commercial bankers, venture capitalists, etc.) like about their jobs? What would they like to change?

- What is the future of the industry for the next few years? How will the industry change? How will the margins change? The return on equity?

- What is the career track in the industry? What skills are required at what stage?

- What is so exciting about this job?

- What is the culture of an I-banking firm as compared to, say, a Fortune 500 company? Compared with a startup?

- What are the exit opportunities after 10 years in the industry? After two years?

Research individual firms

Once you've answered questions about the industry, you should begin to narrow your research to specific firms — both to know which firms to target, and to be knowledgeable for your interviews. Good sources for research are easily accessible publications like *The Wall Street Journal*, *Business Week* and *Fortune*. If you have the resources (perhaps at a school library), you can also read through recent issues of trade publications like *Investment Dealer's Digest*. Vault.com compiles 50-page employer profiles on leading investment banks and other financial services firms specifically for this purpose.

Insiders at business school who have gone through the recruiting rigmarole suggest that you form research and interview practice teams. There is a lot of material to cover, and it is not possible to do it all by yourself. Form teams for researching industries and firms. Later, you can use the same teams to practice interviews. If you are an undergraduate, you should try to see if your school has an investment banking or finance club. If you are in business school, your school will undoubtedly have such a club, or you may want to team up with folks in your cohort who are looking into finance careers. Teams of four to six work quite well for this research process.

Practice your interviews

As you read this guide, you should prepare answers to common questions given at finance interviews — whether they be fit questions, technical questions, or brainteasers. While this may be easiest for technical questions and brainteasers (after all, we can help you to nail those questions with the right answers), it is also important to prepare for fit questions even if there are no right or wrong answers. We can steer you onto the right path with these questions, but you'll need to fill in the blanks. What's the hardest thing you've ever had to do? Can you give me an example of a time when you came up with a creative solution? You don't want to be cursing yourself after an interview, thinking about what you should have said, or examples you could have brought up.

One of the best ways to prepare answers to these questions is to use mock/practice interviews. You can practice by role-playing with your friends and classmates, or by taking advantage of interview training offered by your school. Most MBA career centers, and many undergraduate career centers, offer students the opportunity to perform mock interviews, which are normally videotaped. These practice sessions are conducted either by professional career counselors or by second-year students. The mock interviewees are given the videotape of their critique to watch at home (again and again). Students may choose what kind of interview they'd like to receive: finance, consulting, etc.

What mistakes are commonly unearthed by the videotaped interview? One business school career counselor says that he finds that "most MBAs don't have their story down. They can't elaborate why they came to business school, and why they want to work in the industry." The best candidates are able to describe their background and career history, and make a pitch about why they are interested in a firm, all in a minute or less, career counselors say. Another problem is that many students apparently "can't elaborate their strengths. They have them, but can't sell them. They are too modest." While there's no use demurring when explicating your good points, career center professionals warn that "there is also a danger of tooting your horn too much" — so make sure you're not making any claims for competency you can't back up with relevant experience.

To take full advantage of their mock interviews, career counselors say, students should take them as seriously as possible. Dress professionally "to get into the interviewing mindset." Afterwards, the interviewer will go over the session, assessing the candidate's strengths and weaknesses. It's a good idea to take notes on this feedback.

Mock interviewers also coach students on appropriate answers. "For example," explains one mock interviewer, "many candidates are asked to name their top three weaknesses. Answering with your actual weaknesses is not a good idea. So when I identify a student's weaker point — maybe they are weak on real teamwork experience — we strategize on an appropriate answer. It's better to say something like 'I wouldn't call them weaknesses, but there are three areas in which I still have room to grow,' and then choose three areas that are not deal-breakers."

Do interviewers thus end up hearing the same canned answers over and over again? "I do hear from some interviewers at certain schools — not mine! — that they do hear identical answers to certain questions," says one insider. "My advice to students is to always put answers into their own words."

Prepare questions

Finally, don't forget that finance interviewers often ask candidates whether they have any questions. Don't get caught looking like a job applicant who hasn't done research and is not curious about the opportunities. Read about the firms, read about the industries, and prepare some intelligent questions.

Questions

1. Why do you want to do investment banking/investment management/whatever career you plan to pursue?

If you do not have a finance background, or are an undergrad, this is a question you are guaranteed to receive. Don't say that you wanted to be an I-banker all your life (unless you want to assure yourself a "ding"), but do talk about how your experiences have prepared you for an I-banking job. Talk about how you have developed the core skills required to be in finance (analytical ability, good communication skills, oh — and don't forget, hardworking).

2. Walk me through your resume.

Again, highlight those activities and previous positions that are most applicable to the core finance skills. You should also talk about the things you are proud of and that set you apart.

3. Why should we hire you?

When answering an open-ended question like this, try to make them insightful and entertaining like you did for your school applications. As you prepare your answers to the interview questions, think of them as if they were speeches. What would your stories and anecdotes be? Would they be exciting? Funny? Insightful? Absorbing? Something that the audience would remember for a long time? Unique?

Also, use this as an opportunity to show your interviewers that you have the makeup for the position: hardworking, analytical, team-oriented. Prepare examples to bolster this claim.

4. Why did you decide to do an MBA?

If you are an MBA student looking for a finance position, you are probably going to get this question. If you came from a finance background, you can talk about how you thought you would add to your skill set by going to business school, and how that expectation has panned out.

5. What types of activities did you pursue while in college?

While it may be all good and well to talk about the soup kitchen, remember that you're interviewing for intense, stressful positions. Says one interviewer, "We love to see people who worked part-time, went to all six of their classes, got As and don't seem to need sleep. Frankly, banks like people in debt who will kill themselves for the big bonus. I believe 'hungry' people are highly valued in the interview process." (That's not what we meant by the soup kitchen!)

6. Why are you applying to this firm?

Get ready to talk about the industry and the firm specifically. For some firms (smaller, specialized I-banks like Lazard Freres or Wasserstein Perella, for example), this is an especially important question. Says one insider at a boutique firm, "You definitely want to have someone who knows what they're getting into. I don't think its advisable to say I'm looking at all the bulge-bracket firms — plus [yours]. You want to see people who are very focused." And even at those big firms that all seem the same, your interviewer will be impressed and flattered if you can talk about how his or her firm is different and why that interests you.

7. Give me an example of a project that you've done that involved heavy analytical thinking.

Candidates without a financial background should have an answer prepared for this question that describes a work or school project, focusing on the part that required a lot of number crunching.

8. Give me an example of a time you worked as part of a team.

You're sure to get this one. Draw on experiences from previous work experience, from volunteer activities, and any other situation in which you worked toward a common goal. Highling your strengths as a team member: empathy, collaboration, consensus-building, etc.

Vault.com Guide to Finance Interviews

Introduction

9. What is the most striking thing you've read recently in *The Wall Street Journal*?

A variation of this question is: "What publications do you read regularly?." With these questions, your interviews want to see how well read you are and how well you can describe any of the recent burning financial issues. Read the *Journal* regularly, especially when it is close to the interview time. We suggest starting with 45 minutes a day and gradually bringing that down as you become more efficient in your information-gathering.

10. Describe a project you have worked on that you enjoyed.

Another opportunity to show that you are a hardworking, responsible, analytical team player.

11. Let me give you a situation: "It is Friday afternoon. Tomorrow morning you have to catch a flight to Boston for your best friend's marriage, and you are in the wedding. You have informed your deal team well in advance and they know that you will be gone. Just when you are about to leave, you find out that client wants to meet with the banking team tomorrow. What will you do?"

One of the big things assets you bring to a finance position, especially those with investment banks, is your attitude towards work. This is a rather tricky question, but use this to express the fact that you understand the hardships that an I-banking career would involve, and that you have endured such sacrifice situations previously.

12. Say you are supposed to meet your girlfriend for dinner but the MD asks you to stay late. What do you do? Can you give me an example of a similar situation you have faced before?

Another attitude question. Be prepared.

13 Let's say I give you this summer job/full-time job today. Now let's move to the future and say that at the end of the summer, you find out that you did not get a full-time offer, or that six months into the job you are fired. Give me three reasons why this could happen, and what you can do to prevent this.

This is a twist on the "So what are your weaknesses" question, made specifically more stressful for the finance interview. Don't lose your cool, and have answers prepared for the "weaknesses" question.

14 Think of a person you feel knows you very well both professionally and socially. If I were to call this person and ask him to describe you, what would he say?

Another twist on a personal question designed to get you talking about your strengths and weaknesses.

15 What motivates you?

Think through this one. First of all, you should indicate that you are highly motivated. Second, remember the profile that finance interviews are generally looking for.

16 Can you give me an example of an experience of failure?

You should have an answer prepared for this question. Be modest and admit that you have experienced setbacks. Also, focus on how you bounced back from this setback and what you learned from the experience.

17 You don't seem like you are a very driven person, how will you be able to handle a job in banking?

A stress personal question that can easily hit you during the long and tiring interview process. For example, interviewing with Goldman, you might meet with more than a dozen people in a day. In this situation, it is very easy to appear worn out, which is precisely what you have to convince them that you don't wear out easily. Come up with a good example of a time when you were totally driven.

18. Tell me about an accomplishment that you are proud of.

This is your chance to shine. Remember: teamwork, analytic ability, hardworking, dependable.

19. Can you tell me about a time when you handled many things at the same time?

In some finance positions, especially I-banking, multi-tasking is an important attribute. Think through your background and prepare for this question.

20. What would you like for me to tell you?

Remember, you will be asked for questions yourself. Do your research and impress your interviewer with your knowledge and insight.

Valuation Techniques

Imagine yourself to be CEO of a publicly traded company that makes widgets. You've had a greatly successful business so far and want to sell the company to anyone interested in buying it. How do you know how much to sell it for? Likewise, consider the recent AOL-Netscape acquisition. How did AOL decide how much it should pay to buy Netscape?

For starters, we should understand that the value of a company is equal to the value of its assets, and that

$$\text{Value of Assets} = \text{Debt} + \text{Equity}$$

or

$$\text{Assets} = D + E$$

If I buy a company, I buy its stock (equity) and assume its debt (bonds and loans). Buying a company's equity means that I actually gain ownership of the company — if I buy 50% of a company's equity, I own 50% of the company. Assuming a company's debt means that I promise to pay the company's lenders the amount owed by the previous owner.

The value of debt is easy to calculate: the market value of debt is equal to the book value of debt. (If in the books it says that a company owes its bondholders $1 million, that's how much that debt is worth in the market.) Figuring out the market value of equity is trickier, and that's where valuation techniques come into play.

The four most commonly used techniques are:

1. Discounted cash flow (DCF) analysis

2. Comparable transactions method

3. Multiples method

4. Market valuation

Basic Accounting Concepts

Before we look at these valuation techniques, let's take a look at basic accounting concepts that underpin valuation. MBAs interested in finance careers should definitely be comfortable with these concepts (and may find this overview to be very basic). Undergrads who have taken accounting classes should already be familiar with these concepts as well.

Basic overview of financial statements

There are four basic financial statements that provide financial statement users with the information they need to evaluate a company:

- Balance Sheets
- Income Statements
- Statements of Retained Earnings
- Statements of Cash Flows

These four statements are provided in the annual reports published by public companies. In addition, a company's annual report is almost always accompanied by notes to the financial statements. The notes provide additional information about the numbers provided in the four basic financial statements.

The next four sections provide a general overview of the four basic financial statements.

The Balance Sheet

The **Balance Sheet** presents the financial position of a company at a given point in time. It is comprised of three parts: Assets, Liabilities, and Equity. Assets are the economic resources of a company. They are the resources that the company uses to operate its business and include Cash, Inventory, and Equipment (accounts in financial statements are capitalized). A company normally obtains the resources it uses to operate its business by incurring debt, obtaining new investors, or through operating earnings. The Liabilities section of the Balance Sheet presents the debts of the company. Liabilities are the claims that creditors have on the company's resources. The Equity section of the Balance Sheet presents the net worth of a company, which equals the assets that the company owns less the debts they owe to creditors. Equity can also be defined as the claims that investors have on the company's resources.

This example uses the basic format of a Balance Sheet:

Media Entertainment, Inc
Balance Sheet
December 31, 1998

Assets		Liabilities	
Cash	203,000	Accounts Payable	7,000
Accounts Receivable	26,000		
Building	19,000	**Equity**	
		Common Stock	10,000
		Retained Earnings	231,000
Total Assets	248,000	**Total Liabilities & Equity**	248,000

Because a company can obtain resources from both investors and creditors, one must be able to distinguish between the two and understand why one type is classified as a Liability and the other type is classified as Equity. Companies incur debt to obtain the economic resources necessary to operate their businesses and promise to pay the debt back over a specified period of time. This promise to pay is fixed and is not based upon the operating performance of the company. Companies also seek new investors to obtain economic resources. However, they don't promise to pay investors back a specified amount over a specified period of time. Instead, companies promise investors a return on their investment that is often contingent upon a certain level of operating performance. Since an equity holder's investment is not guaranteed, it is more risky in nature that a loan made by a creditor. But if a company performs well, the return to investors is often higher. The "promise-to-pay" element makes loans made by creditors a Liability and, as an accountant would say, more "senior" than equity holdings.

To summarize, the Balance Sheet represents the economic resources of a business, including the claims that creditors and equity holders have on those resources. Debts owed to creditors are more senior than the investments of equity holders and are classified as Liabilities, while equity investments are accounted for in the Equity section of the Balance Sheet.

The Income Statement

We have discussed two of the three ways in which a company normally obtains the economic resources necessary to operate its business: by incurring debt and by seeking new investors. A third way in which a company can obtain resources is through its own operations. The **Income Statement** presents the results of operations of a business over a specified period of time (e.g. one year, one quarter, one month) and is composed of Revenues, Expenses, and Net Income. Revenue is a source of income that normally arises from the sale of goods or services that the company is in business to sell and is recorded when it is earned. For example, when a retailer of roller blades makes a sale, the sale would be considered revenue. However, income may also come from other sources. For example, selling a business segment or a piece of capital equipment generates a type of revenue for a company. This type of income would be considered a Gain on Sale. Gains are sources of income from peripheral or incidental transactions (i.e. all economic events that are not usual and frequent).

Expenses: Expenses are the costs incurred by a business over a specified period of time to generate the revenues earned during that same period of time. For example, in order for a manufacturing company to sell a product, it must buy the materials it needs to make the product. In addition, that same company must pay people to both make and sell the product. The company must also pay salaries to the individuals who operate the business. These are all types of expenses that a company can incur during the normal operations of the business. When a company incurs an expense outside of its normal operations, it is considered a "loss." Losses are expenses incurred as a result of one-time or incidental transactions. The destruction of office equipment in a fire, for example, would be a loss.

Incurring expenses and acquiring assets both involve the use of economic resources (i.e. cash or debt). So when is a purchase considered an asset and when is it considered an expense?

Assets vs. expenses: A purchase is considered an asset if it provides future economic benefit to the company, while expenses only relate to the current period. For example, monthly salaries paid to employees are for services that they already provided to the company during the month and would be considered expenses. On the other hand, the purchase of a piece of manufacturing equipment would be classified as an asset, as it will probably be used to manufacture a product for more than one accounting period.

Net income: The Revenue a company earns, less its Expenses a specified period of time, equals its Net Income. A positive Net Income number indicates a profit, while a negative Net Income number indicates that a company suffered a loss (called a "net loss").

Here is an example of an Income Statement:

Media Entertainment, Inc
Income Statement
(For the year ended December 31, 1998)

Revenues		
Services Billed		100,000
Expenses		
Salaries and Wages	(33,000)	
Rent Expense	(17,000)	
Utilities Expense	(7,000)	(57,000)
Net Income		43,000

To summarize, the Income Statement measures the success of a company's operations; it provides investors and creditors with information to determine the profitability and creditworthiness of the enterprise. A company has earned net income when its total revenues exceed its total expenses. A company has a net loss when total expenses exceed total revenues.

The Statement of Retained Earnings

The **Statement of Retained Earnings** is a reconciliation of the Retained Earnings account from the beginning to the end of the year. When a company announces income or declares dividends, this information is reflected in the Statement of Retained Earnings. Net income increases the Retained Earnings account. Net losses and dividend payments decrease Retained Earnings.

Here is an example of a basic Statement of Retained Earnings:

Media Entertainment, Inc
Statement of Retained Earnings
(For the year ended December 31, 1998)

Retained Earnings, January 1, 1998	$200,000
Plus: Net income for the year	43,000
	243,000
Less: Dividends declared	(12,000)
Retained Earnings, December 31, 1998	$ 231,000

As you can probably tell by looking at this example, the Statement of Retained Earnings doesn't provide any new information not already reflected in other financial statements. But it does provide additional information about what management is doing with the company's earnings. Management may be "plowing back" the company's net income into the business by retaining part or all of its earnings, distributing its current income to shareholders, or distributing current and accumulated income to shareholders. (Investors can use this information to align their investment strategy with the strategy of a company's management. An investor interested in growth and returns on capital may be more inclined to invest in a company that "plows back" its resources into the company for the purpose of generating additional resources. Conversely, an investor interested in receiving current income is more inclined to invest in a company that pays quarterly dividend distributions to shareholders.)

The Statement of Cash Flows

Remember that the Income Statement provides information about the economic resources involved in the operation of a company. However, the Income Statement does not provide information about the actual source and use of cash generated during its operations. That's because obtaining and using economic resources doesn't always involve cash. For example, let's say you went shopping and bought a new mountain bike on your credit card in July – but didn't pay the bill until August. Although the store did not receive cash in July, the sale would still be considered July revenue. The **Statement of Cash Flows** presents a detailed summary of all of the cash inflows and outflows during the period and is divided into three sections based on three types of activity:

- Cash flows from operating activities: includes the cash effects of transactions involved in calculating net income

- Cash flows from investing activities: involves items classified as assets in the Balance Sheet and includes the purchase and sale of equipment and investments

- Cash flows from financing activities: involves items classified as liabilities and equity in the Balance Sheet; it includes the payment of dividends as well as issuing payment of debt or equity

The example on the next page shows the basic format of the Statement of Cash Flows.

Valuation Techniques

Media Entertainment, Inc
Statement of Cash Flows
For the year ended December 31, 1998

Cash flows provided from operating activities		
Net Income		33,000
Depreciation Expense		10,000
Increase in Accounts Receivable	(26,000)	
Increase in Accounts Payable	7,000	(19,000)
Net cash provided by operating activities		24,000
Cash flows provided from investing activities		
Purchase of Building	(19,000)	
Sale of Long-Term Investment	35,000	
Net cash provided by investing activities		16,000
Cash flows provided from financing activities		
Payment of Dividends	(12,000)	
Issuance of Common Stock	10,000	
Net cash provided by financing activities		(2,000)
Net increase (decrease) in cash		38,000
Cash at the beginning of the year		165,000
Cash at the end of the year		203,000

As you can tell be looking at the above example, the Statement of Cash Flows gets its information from all three of the other financial statements:

- Net income from the Income Statement is shown in the section "cash flows from operating activities."

- Dividends from the Statement of Retained Earnings is shown in the section "cash flows from financing activities."

- Investments, Accounts Payable, and other asset and liability accounts from the Balance Sheet are shown in all three sections.

Market Valuation

Now let's look at the major techniques of valuation. We'll begin with market valuation, as it is the simplest way to value a publicly traded firm. A publicly traded firm is one that is registered on a stock exchange (like the New York Stock Exchange or NASDAQ). The company's stock can be bought and sold on that exchange. Most companies we are familiar with, such as The Coca-Cola Company, IBM, and General Motors, are publicly traded. Every publicly traded company is required to publish an annual report, which includes financial figures such as annual revenues, income, and expenses. The 10Ks and 10Qs for publicly traded firms are available online through the SEC Edgar database, www.edgar-online.com.

The value of a publicly traded firm is easy to calculate. All you need to do is find the company's stock price (the price of a single share), multiply it by the number of shares outstanding, and then – voilá – you have the equity market value of the company. (This is also known as market capitalization or "market cap.") The market price of a single share of stock is readily available from publications like *The Wall Street Journal* and from various quote services available on the Internet today; the number of shares outstanding can be obtained from the annual report of the company.

Example:

Company A stock price	$60/share
# of shares outstanding	200 million
Equity Market Value (market cap)	= $60 x 200 million = $12 billion

Once you determine the market value of a firm, you need to figure out either the discount or premium that it would sell for. When a company sells for a discount it is selling for a value lower than the market value; when it sells for a premium, it is selling for a value greater than the market value. Whether a company sells at a premium or a discount depends on those supply and demand forces you learned about in Econ 101. Typically, if someone wants to acquire a firm, it will sell for a price above the market value of the firm. This is referred to as an acquisition premium. If the acquisition is a hostile takeover, or if there is an auction, the premiums are pushed even higher. The premiums are decided by the perception of the synergies resulting from the purchase or merger. (See section on M&A.)

Discounted Cash Flow (DCF)

The DCF analysis is the most thorough way to value a company, and second-year MBAs should expect to be tested on their ability to do a DCF in a finance interview. There are two ways to value a company using the DCF approach: the Adjusted Present Value (APV) method and the Weighted Average Cost of Capital (WACC) Method. Both methods require calculation of the free cash flows (FCF) of a company and the net present value (NPV) of these FCFs. Before we look at these methods, we'll examine their underlying concepts: net present value, the Capital Asset Pricing Model (CAPM), free cash flows, and terminal year value.

Net Present Value

What do we mean when we talk about **net present value**? We'll explain this important concept with a simple example. Let's say you had an arrangement under which you were set to receive $20 from a friend one year from now. Now let's say for some reason that you decide you don't want to wait for a year and would rather have the money today. How much should you be willing to accept today? More than $20, $20, or less than $20?

Perhaps the reason you would rather have the money today is that you are worried about the likelihood of your receiving the money a year from now. What if, in the next year, your friend goes bankrupt, decides to pretend he does not remember the arrangement, or something else happens that makes him unable to return the money?

Because of this risk, you should be just as happy if you were to receive an amount slightly below $20 today. The rule of thumb for net present value is this: "Money today is worth more than the same money tomorrow." (We might recall the sly Wimpy, who, with an apparent understanding of this rule, tries to convince Popeye that "I will gladly pay you Tuesday for a hamburger today.")

How much lower you should be willing to go if you don't want to wait until next year to receive your $20? That depends on what your estimate of the risk associated is. Thus we have the concept of the "**discount rate**," which is the rate you are willing to discount the future cash flow of $20. Discount rate can also be understood as the expected return from a project of a certain amount of risk.

Note: The "discount rate" is different than the "opportunity cost" of the money. Opportunity cost is a measure of the opportunity lost. Discount rate is a measure of the risk. These are two separate concepts.

To express the relationship between the present value and future value, we use the following formula:

$$\text{Present Value} = \frac{\text{Future Value}}{(1 + r_d)^n}$$

Here, "r_d" is the discount rate, and "n" is the number of years in the future.

The method of calculating the discount rate is different depending on the method of valuation used (i.e. APV method vs. WACC method). Although the discount rate varies, the concept of NPV, or net present value, is the same.

Let's say a series of cash flows is expressed as the following:

Year	1	2	3	4	5	6	7	8
Free Cash Flows	FCF_1	FCF_2	FCF_3	FCF_4	FCF_5	FCF_6	FCF_7	FCF_8

Net present value (NPV) in Year 0 of future cash flows is calculated with the following formula:

$$NPV = \frac{FCF_1}{(1+r_d)^1} + \frac{FCF_2}{(1+r_d)^2} + \frac{FCF_i}{(1+r_d)^i} + \frac{FCF_8}{(1+r_d)^8}$$

or

$$NPV = \sum_{i=1}^{n} \left(\frac{FCF_i}{(1+r_d)^i} \right)$$

Here again, r_d is the discount rate, which is calculated differently depending on whether you use APV or WACC (to be explained later).

Note: In Microsoft Excel, the commonly used spreadsheet software for these purposes, there is a function "= NPV(r_d, cash flow range ID)" which can be used to easily calculate Net Present Value.

CAPITAL ASSET PRICING MODEL (CAPM)

In order to find the appropriate "discount rate" used to discount the company's cash flows, you use the **Capital Asset Pricing Model**, or ("CAPM"). This is a model used to calculate the expected return on your investment, also referred to as expected return on equity, r_e. It is a linear model with one independent variable, Beta. **Beta** represents relative volatility of the given investment with respect to the market. For example, if the Beta of an investment is 1, the returns on the investment (stock/bond/portfolio) vary identically with the market returns. (A Beta less than 1, like 0.5, means the investment is less volatile than the market. So if the Dow Jones Industrial Average goes up or down 20% the next day, a less volatile stock i.e. (ß < 1) might go up 10% and down 10%, respectively. A Beta of greater than 1, like 1.5, means the investment is more volatile than the market.) A company in a volatile industry, like, say, an Internet company, would be expected to have a Beta greater than 1. A company whose value does not vary much, like an electric utility, would be expected to have a Beta under 1. Here, "the market" refers to a well-diversified index like the Dow Jones Industrials Average or the S&P 500.

Mathematically, CAPM is calculated as

$$r_e = r_f + \beta(r_m - r_f)$$

Here:

r_e = Discount rate for an all-equity firm

r_f = Risk-free rate (The Treasury bill rate for the period the cash projections are being considered. For example, if we are considering a 10-year period, then the risk-free rate is the rate for the 10-year U.S. Treasury note.)

$r_m - r_f$ = Excess market return (This is the excess annual return of the stock market over a U.S. Treasury bond over a long period of time. This is usually assumed to be 7% for the U.S. Market.)

β = Equity Beta

Equity Beta is given in various sources like Value Line. These days, Yahoo also carries the equity Beta of publicly traded firms. If the firm you are valuing is not publicly traded, then you need to get a firm with a similar Balance Sheet and Income Statement that is publicly traded. (When calculating CAPM you should be careful to use the "equity Beta" value, and not "assets Beta.") If you have information for Beta assets rather than Beta equity, you can derive Beta equity using the following relationship:

$$\beta_A = (\beta_E)\frac{(E)}{(D+E)} + (1-t)\frac{(D)}{(D+E)}(\beta_D)$$

Here:

D = Market value of debt (usually the book value of debt)

E = Market value of equity (the number of shares outstanding x share price) (Also known as "market cap.")

β_D = Beta debt (usually one can assume this to be equal to 0)

t = Corporate taxes, (usually assumed to be 35%)

Therefore:

$$\beta_E = \beta_A \frac{(D + E)}{(E)}$$

Free cash flows

To capture the characteristics of an all-equity firm we recalculate a company's cash flows as if there were no debt in the firm. The free cash flow (FCF) of an all-equity firm in year (i) can be calculated as:

$$FCF_i = \text{Earnings Before Interest and Taxes} \times (1 - t)$$
$$+ \text{Depreciation \& Amortization}$$
$$- \text{Capital Expenditure ("CapEx")}$$
$$- \text{Net increase in working capital}$$
$$+ \text{Other relevant cash flows for an all equity firm}$$

Here:

Earnings Before Interest and Taxes (or EBIT) can be obtained from the Income Statement (see section on major accounting concepts).

t = Corporate tax rate, usually assumed to be 35%.

Depreciation & Amortization of a firm can be obtained from the firm's Balance Sheet (see section on major accounting concepts).

Capital Expenditure and Net increase in working capital can be obtained from the Statement of Cash Flows.

Other relevant cash flows for an all-equity firm would be items like asset sale proceeds (selling a major piece of real estate, for example) or the use of tax loss carry-forwards or tax credits.

Terminal Year Calculation

The terminal year represents the year (usually 10 years in the future) when the growth of the company can be considered to have stabilized.

In other words...

The cash flows of the first 10 years are determined by company management or a financial analyst, based on predictions and forecasts of what will happen. Then, a terminal year value needs to be calculated assuming that after year 10 the cash flows of the company keep growing at the given rate, represented as "g."

The value of the terminal year cash flows (that is, the value in year 10) is given by:

$$\text{TY FCF} = \frac{FCF_{10}(1+g)}{(r_d - g)}$$

The present value of the terminal year cash flows (that is, the value today) is given by:

$$\text{PV (TY FCF)} = \frac{\text{TY FCF}}{(1+r_d)^{10}}$$

or

$$\text{PV (TY FCF)} = \frac{FCF_{10}(1+g)}{(1+r_d)^{10}(r_d - g)}$$

Adding it up

Adding the value of the terminal year free cash flows (TY FCF) and future cash flows (FCFs) up to the terminal year gives us the value of the company under the DCF analysis. These cash flows need to be discounted to the present using methods discussed in the net present value calculations.

Calculating discount rates

Remember when we said that there are several ways of calculating discount rates? We'll now look at the two most popular methods of discounted cash flow (DCF) analysis tested in finance interviews: the WACC (Weighted Average Cost of Capital) and APV (Adjusted Present Value). The key difference between the two methods is the way in which the discount rate is calculated. For WACC, we calculate the discount rate for leveraged equity (r_e^L); for APV, we calculate the dicount rate for an all-equity firm (r_e^U).

WACC

For WACC, the discount rate is calculated with the following formula:

$$r_{dWACC} = \frac{(E)}{(D+E)} (r_e^L) + \frac{(D)}{(D+E)} (1-t)(r_D)$$

Here:

D = Market value of debt

E = Market value of equity

r_D = Discount rate for debt = Average interest rate on long-term debt

r_e^L = Discount rate for (leveraged) equity (calculated using the CAPM)

Note: The terms (E)/(D + E) and (D)/(D + E) represent the "target" equity and debt ratios (also referred to as the equity-to-debt and debt-to-equity ratios).

$$\text{CAPM:}$$
$$r_e^L = r_f + \beta^L (r_m - r_f)$$

Here:

r_f = Risk-free rate = the Treasury bond rate for the period for which the projections are being considered

$r_m - r_f$ = Excess market return

β^L = Leveraged Beta

Finding the value of leveraged Beta from unleveraged Beta can be calculated from the unleveraged Beta using the equation below, in a process also referred to as "unlevering the Beta":

$$\beta^L = \beta^U \left[1 + (1-t)\frac{(D)}{(E)} \right]$$

Here:

β^U = Unleveraged Beta (This can be obtained from Value Line or online sources like Yahoo!)

APV

For the APV calculation the discount rate is calculated with the following formula:

$$r_e^U = r_f + \beta^U (r_m - r_f)$$

Here:

β^U = Unleveraged Beta

Thus we see that the key difference between WACC and APV is that in the APV calculation, we take the unleveraged equity discount rate, rather than a leveraged (historical) discount rate. The APV caluclation assumes an "all-equity" firm, rather than one with debt.

To summarize:

Method	Discount Rate	Type of Firm (Assumption)	Beta
APV	r_e^U	all equity	β^U
WACC	r_e^L	leveraged/historical	β^L

To compensate for this difference we add a value for the debt tax shield separately to arrive at an overall valuation of the company. The debt tax shield (DTS) for any year is given by:

$$DTS = (t)(r_D)(D)$$

Here:

D = Total debt for the company that year

r_D = Weighted average interest rate on that debt calculated for each year of the projected cash flows

t = Corporate tax rate

The debt tax shield captures the value added by debt. The interest paid on the debt reduces the total taxes being paid. This principle is the main reason for the emergence of the LBO (leveraged buyout) shops, including the famous KKR takeover of RJR Nabisco that inspired the bestseller *Barbarians at the Gate*. KKR borrowed money (introduced debt) to buy RJR Nabisco at a price way above the market price. Since the company had no debt before the takeover and highly reliable cash flows, KKR was able to increase the value of the company by financial restructuring.

The tricky question now is: What discount rate should be used for calculating the present value of the DTS? The answer is the discount rate that would best capture the risk associated with the DTS. If you assume that the ability to use the tax shield is as risky as the cash flows to an all-equity firm, we would use the r_e^U. If you assume that the tax shield is as risky as the ability to repay the debt, then the discount rate should be the average interest rate, or r_D.

Note: The debt tax shield is similarly calculated for the terminal year and discounted to the present year.

One simple approximation for the DTS that can be used for most back-of-the-envelope calculations in an interview is:

$$\text{APV with DTS} = \frac{\text{APV without DTS}}{(1 - t)(L)}$$

Here:

t = Tax rate

L = Leverage ratio (also referred to as the long-term debt ratio) = $D/(D + E)$

The main difference between the WACC and APV methods is that the WACC takes the "target" debt-to-equity ratio to calculate the discount rate. However, the target debt-to-equity ratio is not reached until a few years in the future. Hence the method is not "academically complete." The APV method takes this into consideration and looks at an "all-equity" firm.

However, the difference that amounts from assuming a target debt-to-equity ratio is very small; most investment banks use the WACC method even though most business schools teach both methods. The difference between the two methods will become clearer as we go through an example.

Step one – Assumptions

You are given the following information for the company you are valuing:

	Year One	Year Two	Year Three	Year Four
EBIT	7.0	7.5	7.9	8.4
Depreciation	2.9	2.7	2.7	2.6
Capital Expenditures	1.5	2.5	2.5	3.0
Increase in Working Capital	0.8	1.5	1.5	0.9

Tax Rate (t)	35%
Book Value Debt (D)	7.0
Book Value Equity (E_{book})	10.0
Market Value Equity (E_{market})	15.0
Beta (historical) (β_L)	1.5
Long-term T-Bond rate (r_f)	10.0%
Long-term debt rate (r_D)	12.0%
Long-term growth rate (g)	6.0%
Long-term risk premium ($r_m - r_f$)	8.0%

Step two – Cash Flows

Free cash flow to all equity firm = EBIT (1 - t) + Depr. - CAPX - Ch NWC.

Plugging in our data, we get:

Year One   = 7.0 (1 - 0.35) + 2.9 - 1.5 - 0.8 = 5.15
Year Two   = 7.5 (1 - 0.35) + 2.7 - 2.5 - 1.5 = 3.58
Year Three = 7.9 (1 - 0.35) + 2.7 - 2.5 - 1.5 = 3.84
Year Four = 8.4 (1 - 0.35) + 2.6 - 3.0 - 0.9 = 4.16

So our free cash flows look like this:

	Year One	Year Two	Year Three	Year Four
FCF	5.15	3.58	3.84	4.16

Step three – Discount Rates

APV

Remember that there are two ways to determine a discount rate. Let's begin with the APV analysis

First get β^U from the β^L of 1.50

$$\beta^U = \frac{\beta^L}{\left[1 + (1-t)\frac{(D)}{E_{(market\ value)}}\right]}$$

$$\beta^U = \frac{1.50}{\left[1 + (1-0.35)\frac{(7.0)}{(15.0)}\right]} = 1.15$$

$$r_e^U = r_f + \beta^U(r_m - r_f)$$

$$r_e^U = 0.10 + (1.15)(0.08) = \mathbf{0.0192\ or\ 19.2\%}$$

Hence, the expected return on equity for an all-equity firm would be 19.2%. We will use this as the discount rate for the APV analysis.

Remember:

β^L = Beta for a firm with debt, or historical Beta (leveraged/historical Beta)

β^U = Beta for the equivalent firm without debt, or an all-equity firm (unleveraged Beta)

WACC

Let's now look at the WACC method. For WACC, we need to know what the target (long-term) debt-to-capital ratio for this company is. Let's assume that it is 40%. That is, in the long run, this company expects to finance its projects with 40% debt and 60% equity.

First, we need to calculate β^L

$$\beta^L = \beta^U \left[1 + (1 - t) \frac{(D)}{(E)} \right]$$

$$\beta^L = 1.15 \left[1 + (1 - 0.35) \frac{(0.4)}{(0.6)} \right]$$

$$= 1.64$$

$$r_e^L = r_f + \beta^L (r_m + r_f)$$

$$r_e^L = (0.10) + (1.64)(0.08) = \textbf{0.2312 or 23.12\%}$$

Note: Here we calculate our expected return on equity, or r_e^L, using the target debt-to-equity ratio. We use this r_e^L for all years whether or not that target ratio has been matched or not. Since our long-term debt rate is 13.0%, and our long-term debt is 40%, we can now calculate WACC.

$$\text{WACC} = \frac{(E)}{(D+E)} (r_e^L) + \frac{(D)}{(D+E)} (1-t)(r_D)$$

$$= 0.6 \times 0.2312 + 0.4 \times (1 - 0.35) \times 0.13$$

$$= \textbf{0.1725 or 17.3\%}$$

Step four – Terminal Value

We assume that the company operates forever. But, we only have four years of cash flow. We need to put a value on all the cash flows after Year Four. The Year Four cash flow is 4.16 and we expect it to grow at 5% a year. The value of all cash flows after Year Four (as of the end of Year Four) can be calculated with our Terminal Value formula from p. 27.

APV

$$\text{TY FCF} = \frac{FCF_{10}(1+g)}{(r_d - g)}$$

$$\text{TY FCF} = \frac{4.16 \times (1 + 0.05)}{(0.192 - 0.05)} = 30.76$$

WACC

$$\text{TY FCF} = \frac{FCF_{10}(1+g)}{(r_d - g)}$$

$$\text{TY FCF} = \frac{4.16 \times (1 + 0.05)}{(0.173 - 0.05)} = 35.51$$

Step five – Taking the NPV of all the cash flows

Now we have to add up our cash flows

APV

	Year One	Year Two	Year Three	Year Four
FCF	5.15	3.58	3.84	4.16

Add terminal value → 30.76

FCF$_{adjusted}$	5.15	3.58	3.84	34.92

Using these cash flows, and our discount rate of 19.2%, we can calculate the net present value using the formula from p. 24.

$$NPV = \frac{FCF_1}{(1+r_d)^1} + \frac{FCF_2}{(1+r_d)^2} + \frac{FCF_i}{(1+r_d)^i} + \frac{FCF_8}{(1+r_d)^8}$$

$$NPV = \frac{5.15}{(1+0.192)} + \frac{3.58}{(1+0.192)^2} + \frac{3.84}{(1+0.192)^3} + \frac{34.92}{(1+0.192)^4}$$

$$NPV = 4.32 + 2.52 + 2.27 + 17.30 = \mathbf{26.41}$$

Let's add up the cash flows for the WACC method:

WACC

	Year One	Year Two	Year Three	Year Four
FCF	5.15	3.58	3.84	4.16

Add terminal value → 35.51

FCF$_{adjusted}$	5.15	3.58	3.84	39.67

Using these cash flows, with a discount rate of 17.2%, we can calculate an NPV

$$NPV = \frac{FCF_1}{(1+r_d)^1} + \frac{FCF_2}{(1+r_d)^2} + \frac{FCF_i}{(1+r_d)^i} + \frac{FCF_8}{(1+r_d)^8}$$

$$NPV = \frac{5.15}{(1+0.173)} + \frac{3.58}{(1+0.173)^2} + \frac{3.84}{(1+0.173)^3} + \frac{39.67}{(1+0.173)^4}$$

$$NPV = 4.39 + 2.60 + 2.38 + 20.95 = \mathbf{30.3} \text{ (approximately)}$$

Step 6 — Figuring out the Company's Value

For WACC, we are done with our calculation — the value of the company is $30.3.

For APV, however, we add the present value of the interest tax shields. We use the following formula:

$$\text{APV w/ debt tax benefits} = \frac{\text{APV without debt tax benefits}}{(1-t) \times (\text{long-term debt ratio})}$$

If the company's long-term debt ratio is 40%:

$$\text{APV w/ debt tax benefits} = \frac{26.41}{(1-0.35) \times (0.4)}$$

$$= \$30.7$$

Note: This is an approximation. The theoretically complete way would involve calculating the DTS for each year.

To summarize

	APV	WACC
Discounted value of FCF	$26.41	$30.3
Value of tax shield	$4.3	
Total	$30.7	$30.3

The APV and WACC methods make slightly different assumptions about the value of interest tax shields, and we have received slightly different values.

Comparable Transactions

With this technique of valuing a company for a merger or acquisition, you look at transactions that have taken place in the industry that are similar to the transaction under consideration. For example, when NationsBank was considering acquiring Montgomery Securities, it likely studied **comparable transactions**, such as Bankers Trust's acquisition of Alex. Brown or Bank of America's acquisition of Roberston Stephens. In other words, NationsBank looked at other acquisitions of investment banks by financial institutions that had taken place in the recent past.

With the comparable transactions method, you are looking for a key valuation parameter. That is, are the companies in those transactions being valued as a multiple of EBIT, EBITDA, revenue, or some other parameter? If you figure out what the key valuation parameter is, you can examine at what multiples of those parameters the companies are being valued in a series of transactions. You can then value the company similarly.

As an example, let's assume that there is an Internet start-up called echicago.com that is planning to go public. Let's also say that this is a health care Internet company. The question the company's financial management, their investment bankers, and the portfolio managers who are planning to buy stock in the company will ask is: "How much is the company worth?"

To obtain a value for the company, they can look at recent comparable transactions. For example, suppose eharvard.com and estanford.com are other health care Internet companies that have recently successfully gone public. The financials of the companies are summarized below.

Company	Value (Market Cap) (mil)	Sales (mil)	EBITDA (mil)	Earnings (Losses) (mil)	Sales Multiples (Market Cap/Sales)
echicago.com	?	80	20	(10)	?
estanford.com	2100	70	17	(12)	30
eharvard.com	3000	75	18	(8)	40

Because the three companies are in the same industry and have similar financials, the transaction for echicago.com can be valued at multiples similar to those for the other two. The value for echicago.com could be anywhere from 30 x 80 to 40 x 80, i.e. 2,400 to 3,200 millions of dollars, or $2.4 billion to $3.2 billion. (This range in valuation is how bankers would value the company; because of heavy speculation on Internet stocks recently, however, we would not be surprised if valued the company at an even higher price.)

Multiples

Quite often, there is not enough information to be able to determine the valuation using the comparable transactions method. In these cases, you can value a company based on **market valuation multiples**. Examples of these valuation multiples include price/earning multiples (also known as P/E ratios, this method, which compares a company's market capitalization to its annual income, is the most commonly used multiple) EBITDA multiples, and others. When using this method, you look at what multiples are used for other companies in the industry.

Let's look at an example. What is the value of a company in the semiconductor industry that posts annual sales of $180 million, EBITDA of $70 million, and earnings of $40 million (let's call it Wharton Semiconductor). Companies in the semiconductor industry might be valued with sales multiples, earnings multiples or EBITDA multiples. The numbers used for EBITDA or earnings might be figured for the 12 months trailing (the previous 12 months), the last fiscal year, 12 months projected, or the next fiscal year projected. These figures can be obtained from research reports published by various research departments within investment banks or brokerage houses.

Let's assume that there are four semiconductor companies similar to Wharton Semiconductor. An investment bank would perform a "Common Stock Comparison" to determine relevant multiples:

Company	Value (Market Cap)	Sales	EBITDA	Earnings
Chicago Semiconductor	900	220	115	82
Harvard Semiconductor	700	190	90	60
Kellogg Semiconductor	650	280	68	42
Stanford Semiconductor	320	150	45	26

Valuation Techniques

Company	Sales Multiples $\left(\frac{\text{Market Cap}}{\text{Sales}}\right)$	EBITDA Multiples $\left(\frac{\text{Market Cap}}{\text{EBITDA}}\right)$	Price-to-Earnings Multiples $\left(\frac{\text{Market Cap}}{\text{Earnings}}\right)$
Chicago Semiconductor	4.1	7.8	11.0
Harvard Semiconductor	3.7	7.8	11.7
Kellogg Semiconductor	2.3	9.6	15.5
Stanford Semiconductor	2.1	7.1	12.3
AVERAGE	**3.1**	**8.1**	**12.6**

Using the average multiples from the Common Stock Comparison, we can estimate Wharton Semiconductor's value as follows:

Using the sales multiple: Wharton's sales of $180 million x 3.1 (average sales multiple) = $558 million

Using the EBITDA multiple: Wharton's EBITDA of $70 million x 8.1 (average EBITDA multiple) = $567 million

Using the price-to-earnings multiple: Wharton's earnings of $40 million x 12.6 (average price-to-earnings multiple) = $504 million

So using the multiples method, we can estimate the value of Wharton Semiconductor at between $504 and $567 million.

Vault.com Guide to Finance Interviews
Valuation Techniques

Questions

1. What is the difference between the Income Statement and the Statement of Cash Flows?

The Income Statement is a record of Revenues and Expenses while the Statement of Cash Flows records the actual cash that has either come in or left the company. The Statement of Cash Flows has the following categories: Operating Cash Flows, Investing Cash Flows, and Financing Cash Flows.

Interestingly, a company can be profitable as shown in the Income Statement, but still go bankrupt if it doesn't have the cash flow to meet interest payments.

2. What is the link between the Balance Sheet and the Income Statement?

The main link between the two statements is that profits generated in the Income Statement get added to shareholder's equity on the Balance Sheet as Retained Earnings. Also, the debt on the Balance Sheet is used to calculate interest expense.

3. What is the link between the Balance Sheet and the Statement of Cash Flows?

The Statement of Cash Flows starts with the cash balance, which comes from Balance Sheet. Also, to figure out Cash from Operations, you use the changes in Balance Sheet accounts (such as Accounts Payable, Accounts Receivable, etc.). The net increase in cash flow for the year goes back to the Balance Sheet of the next year.

4. What is EBITDA?

Also known as "cash flow," EBITDA is Earnings Before Interest, Taxes, Depreciation, and Amortization.

5. Say you knew a company's net income. How would you figure out its "cash flow"?

A basic answer: You start with the company's net income. Then you add back depreciation and amortization. Then you subtract the company's Capital Expenditures (called "CapEx" for short, this is how much money the company must invest each year on plants and equipment). The number you get is the company's cash flow:

    Net Income

+ Depreciation and Amortization

− Capital Expenditures

= Cash Flow

6. Walk me through the major line items on a Cash Flow statement.

Another question designed to test your accounting skills. The answer: first the Beginning Cash Balance, then Cash from Operations, then Cash from Investing Activities, then Cash from Financing Activities, and finally the Ending Cash Balance.

7. How do you value a company?

This is one of the most popular technical questions of finance interviews. Remember the several ways that we discussed, and good luck. MBAs looking for I-banking or finance in a company positions are sure to get this one.

One basic answer to this question is to discount the company's projected cash flows by a "risk-adjusted discount rate." After projecting the first five or 10 years, you add in a "Terminal Value," which represents the present value of all the future cash flows that are too far into the future to project. You can calculate the Terminal Value in one of two ways: (1) you take the earnings of the last year you projected, say year 10, and multiply it by some market multiple like 20 times earnings, and that's the terminal value; or (2) you take the last year, say year 10, and assume some constant growth rate after that like 10%. The present value of this growing stream of payments after year 10 is the Terminal Value.

For a more advanced answer, discuss the APV and WACC methods of doing a discounted cash flow analysis (DCF analysis).

Finally, you should also mention other methods of valuing a company, including looking at "comparables" – that is, how other similar companies were valued recently as a multiple of their sales, net income, or some other measure.

Note: To figure out what "discount rate" you would use to discount the company's cash flows, tell your interviewer you would use the "Capital Asset Pricing Model" (or "CAPM"). (In a nutshell, CAPM says that the proper discount rate to use is the risk-free interest rate adjusted upwards to reflect this particular company's market risk or "Beta.")

8. The CEO of a $500 million company has called you, her investment banker. She wants to sell the company. She wants to know how much she can expect for the company today.

It might sound different, but this is the same question as No. 7: How do you value a company?

9. What is the formula for the Capital Asset Pricing Model?

The Capital Asset Pricing Model is used to calculate the expected return on your investment. It is a linear model with one independent variable, Beta. Beta for a company is the relative volatility of the given investment with respect to the market, i.e., if Beta is 1, the returns on the investment (stock/bond/portfolio) vary identically with the market. Here "the market" refers to a well diversified index like the Dow Jones Industrials or the S&P 500. The formula for CAPM is as follows:

$$\textbf{CAPM:}$$
$$r_e^L = r_f + \beta^L (r_m - r_f)$$

r_f = Risk-free rate = the Treasury bond rate for the period for which the projections are being considered

$r_m - r_f$ = Excess market return.

β^L = Leveraged Beta.

r_e^L = Discount rate for (leveraged) equity (calculated using the CAPM)

10. Why might there be multiple valuations for a single company?

As this chapter has discussed, there are several different methods by which one can value a company. And even if you use the rigorously academic DCF analysis, the two main methods (the WACC and APV method) make different assumptions about interest tax shields, which can lead to different valuations.

11. How do you calculate the terminal value of a company?

The value of the terminal year cash flows (usually calculated for 10 years in the future) is calculated by calculating the present value of cash flows from the terminal year (in our case, Year 10) continuing forever with the following formula:

$$\text{TY FCF} = \frac{FCF_{10}(1+g)}{(r_d - g)}$$

Here "g" is an assumed growth rate and r_d is the discount rate. (Remember that you could also calculate the terminal value of a company by taking a multiple of terminal year cash flows, and discounting that back to the present to arrrive at an answer. This alternative method might be used in some instances because it is less dependent on the assumed growth rate (g).

12. Why are the P/E multiples for a company in London different than that of the same company in the States?

The P/E multiples can be different in the two countries even if all other factors are constant because of the difference in the way earnings are recorded two countries. Overall market valuations in American markets could be higher than those in the U.K.

13. What are the different multiples that can be used to value a company?

The most commonly used multiple is earnings, thus the often-quoted price-to-earnings (P/E) ratio. Other figures that are used include revenues, EBITDA, EBIT, and book value. Which figure is used depends on the industry. For example, Internet companies are often valued with revenue multiples; this explains why companies that lose money every year can have such high market caps. Companies in the metal and mining industry are valued using EBITDA.

As discussed in the section on valuation, not only should we be aware of what financial figure is being used, we should know what time period the figure used represents: it can be for the previous or projected 12 months, for example, or for the previous or projected fiscal year.

14. How do you get the discount rate for an all-equity firm?

You use the Capital Asset Pricing Model, or CAPM.

15. Can I apply CAPM in Latin American markets?

CAPM was developed for use in the U.S. markets. However, it is presently the only tool available. Hence while it is an approximation, it is a good framework for thinking and analyzing the markets outside U.S. as fundamentally, markets are based on similar principles.

16. How much would you pay for a company with $50 million in revenue and $5 million in profit?

If this is all the information we are given we should use comparable transaction or multiples method to value this company (rather than the DCF method). To use the multiples method, you would prepare a common stock comparison, using comparable companies in the same industry, to get average industry multiples. These numbers would depend on the industry the company is in.

Vault.com Guide to Finance Interviews

Valuation Techniques

17. How do you value a company with NOLs (net operating losses)?

The valuation would be similar as that for a company making profits. We would use the formula to get to the free cash flows. And if the present value of the free cash flows also come out to be negative, the project (or company) is a negative NPV project, and thereby a bad investment. (Typically, the management of a company will be able to show that cash flows become positive before the terminal year!)

18. How would you value a company with no revenue?

First you would make reasonable assumptions about the company's projected revenues (and projected cash flows) for future years. Then you would calculate the Net Present Value of these cash flows.

19. What is Beta?

Beta is the value that represents the volatility of a stock with respect to overall market volatility.

20. How do you unlever a company's Beta?

Unlevering a company's Beta means calculating the Beta under the assumption that it is an all-equity firm. The formula is as follows:

$$\beta^L = \beta^U \left[1 + \frac{(1 - t)(D)}{(E)} \right]$$

21. What is going on with the valuations of Internet companies today?

There probably is no right answer for this (although there might be some wrong answers). Here, the interviewer is trying to see how you think and how creative ideas you can come up with.

22. Do you think these valuations are justified?

Internet valuations today are based on what the investors believe is the future market potential of the Internet companies. As you know, the Internet has changed the way people do business in recent years, and revenues from Internet based advertising and e-commerce are expected to explode. Whether the current valuations are justified, however, is a point of contention.

23. Value the following company given the following information (a written finance interview question):

Step one – Assumptions

You are given the following information for the company you are valuing:

	Year One	Year Two	Year Three	Year Four
EBIT	480.0	530.0	580.0	605.0
Depreciation	145.0	130.0	110.0	100.0
Capital Expenditures	160.0	140.0	130.0	110.0
Increase in Working Capital	25.0	20.0	15.0	12.0

Tax Rate	40%
Book Value Debt	1,200.0
Book Value Equity	1,500.0
Market Value Equity	1,800.0
Beta (historical)	1.10
Long-term T-Bond rate	8.0%
Long-term debt rate	10.0%
Long-term growth rate	4.0%
Long-term risk premium	6.0%

Step two – Cash Flows

Free cash flow to an all-equity firm = EBIT (1 - t) + Depreciation - Capital Expenditures - Increase in Working Capital

Plugging in our data, our free cash flows look like this:

	Year One	Year Two	Year Three	Year Four
FCF	248.00	288.00	313.00	341.00

Step three – Discount Rates

APV

Remember that there are two ways to determine a discount rate. Let's begin with the APV analysis

First, get β^U from the β^L of 1.50

$$\beta^U = \frac{\beta^L}{\left[1 + (1-t)\frac{D}{E_{(market\ value)}}\right]}$$

$$\beta^U = \frac{1.10}{\left[1 + (1 - 0.40)\frac{(1,200)}{(1,800)}\right]} = 0.79$$

$$r_e^U = r_f + \beta^U(r_m - r_f)$$

$$r_e^U = 0.08 + (0.79)(0.06) = 12.7\%$$

The expected return on equity for an all-equity firm would be 12.7%. We will use this as the discount rate for the APV analysis.

WACC

Let's now look at the WACC method. For WACC, we need to know what the target (long-term) debt-to-capital ratio for this company is. Let's assume that it is 30%. That is, in the long run, this company expects to finance its projects with 30% debt and 70% equity.

First, we need to calculate $ß^L$

$$ß^L = ß^U \left[1 + (1-t)\frac{(D)}{(E)}\right]$$

$$ß^L = 0.79 \left[1 + (1-0.40)\frac{(0.3)}{(0.7)}\right]$$

$$= 0.993$$

$$r_e^L = r_f + (ß^L)(0.06)$$

$$r_e^L = (0.08) + (0.993)(0.06) = \mathbf{0.139 \text{ or } 13.9\%}$$

Since our long-term debt rate is 9.93%, and our long-term debt is 30%, we can now calculate WACC.

$$WACC = \frac{(E)}{(D+E)}(r_e^L) + \frac{(D)}{(D+E)}(1-t)(r_D)$$

$$WACC = 0.07 \times 0.139 + 0.3 \times (1-0.4) \times 0.993$$

$$= \mathbf{0.1153 \text{ or } 11.53\%}$$

Step four – Terminal Value

We assume that the company operates forever. But, we only have four years of cash flow. We need to put a value on all the cash flows after Year Four. The Year Four cash flow is 341 and we expect it to grow at 5% a year. The value of all cash flows after Year Four (as of the end of Year Four) can be calculated with our Terminal Value formula.

APV

$$\text{TY FCF} = \frac{FCF_{10}(1+g)}{(r_d - g)}$$

$$\text{TY FCF} = \frac{341(1 + 0.05)}{(0.127 - 0.05)} = 4{,}650.00$$

WACC

$$\text{TY FCF} = \frac{FCF_{10}(1+g)}{(r_d - g)}$$

$$\text{TY FCF} = \frac{341(1 + 0.05)}{(0.1153 - 0.05)} = 5{,}483.15$$

Step five – taking the NPV of all the cash flows

Now we have to add up our cash flows

APV

	Year One	Year Two	Year Three	Year Four
FCF	248.00	288.00	313.00	341.00

Add terminal value → 4,650

	Year One	Year Two	Year Three	Year Four
FCF$_{adjusted}$	248.00	288.00	313.00	4,991

Using these cash flows, and our discount rate of 12.7%, we can calculate the Net Present Value using the formula from p. 29

$$NPV = \frac{FCF_1}{(1+r_d)^1} + \frac{FCF_2}{(1+r_d)^2} + \frac{FCF_i}{(1+r_d)^i} + \frac{FCF_8}{(1+r_d)^8}$$

$$NPV = \frac{248}{(1+0.173)} + \frac{288}{(1+0.173)^2} + \frac{313}{(1+0.173)^3} + \frac{4,991}{(1+0.173)^4}$$

$$NPV = 220 + 226.7 + 218.66 + 3,093.8 = \mathbf{3,759.16}$$

Let's add up the cash flows for the WACC method:

WACC

	Year One	Year Two	Year Three	Year Four
FCF	248.00	288.00	313.00	341.00

Add terminal value → 5,483.15

	Year One	Year Two	Year Three	Year Four
FCF$_{adjusted}$	248.00	288.00	313.00	5,824.15

$$NPV = \frac{FCF_1}{(1+r_d)^1} + \frac{FCF_2}{(1+r_d)^2} + \frac{FCF_i}{(1+r_d)^i} + \frac{FCF_8}{(1+r_d)^8}$$

$$NPV = \frac{248}{(1+0.173)} + \frac{288}{(1+0.173)^2} + \frac{313}{(1+0.173)^3} + \frac{5,824.15}{(1+0.173)^4}$$

$$NPV = 222.36 + 231.53 + 225.6 + 3,764.1 = \mathbf{4,443.62}$$

Step six – Figuring out the Company's Value

For WACC, we are done with our calculation — the value of the company is $4,443.62.

For APV, however, we add the present value of the interest tax shields. We use the following formula:

$$\text{APV w/ debt tax benefits} = \frac{\text{APV without debt tax benefits}}{(1 - t \times \text{long-term debt ratio})}$$

If the company's long-term debt ratio is 30%:

$$\text{APV w/ debt tax benefits} = \frac{3{,}759.16}{(1 - 0.40) \times (0.3)}$$

$$= \$4{,}271.3$$

To summarize

	APV	WACC
Discounted value of FCF	$3,759.16	$4,443.62
Value of tax shield	$512.61	
Total	$4,271.77	$4,443.62

24. Name three companies that are undervalued and tell me why you think they are.

This is a very popular question for equity research and portfolio management jobs. Here you have to do your homework. Study the stocks you like and see make valuations using various methods: DCF, multiples, comparable transactions, etc. Then choose several undervalued (and overvalued) stocks, and be prepared to back up your assessment.

For example, let's say that Coke received some bad PR recently and its stock took a hammering in the market. However, say the earnings of Coke are not expected to decrease significantly because of the negative publicity (or at least that's your analysis). Thus, Coke is trading at relatively lower P/E than Pepsi and others in the industry and is undervalued. This is an example of a line of reasoning you might offer when asked this question (the more thorough and insightful the reasoning, the better). Using some of the techniques discussed earlier and regular readings of the WSJ and other publications will help you formulate real-world examples.

Also, keep in mind that there are no absolute right answers for a question like this: If everyone in the market believed that a stock was undervalued, the price would go up and it wouldn't be undervalued anymore! What the interviewer is looking for is your chain of thought, your ability to communicate that convincingly and your preparation for the interview.

25. Walk me through the major items of an Income Statement

Revenues, expenses, and net income.

26. Which industries are you interested in? What are the multiples that you use for those industries?

As discussed, different industries use different multiples. If you claim interest in a certain industry, you better know how companies in the industry are commonly valued. (Don't answer the first question without knowing the answer to the second!)

Stocks

A remedial lesson

What does the "Inc." after the names of many companies, mean? Not surprisingly, it means that a company is incorporated. There are many forms of incorporation from which a company can choose. With the help of a lawyer, a company files papers/applications in court to define itself as one of these forms. A company can be incorporated as a C Corp, an S Corp, an LLC (Limited Liability Corporation), or a partnership. There are different rules of ownership for each of these forms, and different tax rules.

The incorporation of a company can be regarded as its birth. And when a company is born, it has "equity." This equity is also referred to as **stock**, and refers to ownership in a company. Most people unfamiliar with the finance world equate stock with the running tickers in the "pits" of Wall Street trading floors, and other symbols of publicly traded stock. But we should realize that companies do not have to be publicly traded in order to have stock — they just have to be incorporated and owned.

Equity vs. debt (stock vs. bonds)

Debt and equity make up the assets of a company. **Equity**, or ownership stake, is the volatile part of the firm's assets. The equity of a company is represented by securities called stocks. Here, when we refer to stock, we are actually referring to **common stock**.

Equity has a book value – this is a strictly defined value that can be calculated from the company's Balance Sheet. It also has a market value. The market value of equity or stock for a publicly traded firm can be found in *The Wall Street Journal* or any of the stock quote services available today. (Market value of a company's equity can be understood with the simple formula: stock price x number of shares outstanding [or common stock outstanding] = market value of equity.) The market value of a private company can be estimated using the valuation techniques discussed in the valuation section of this guide. However, any method used to measure either the book value or market value of a company depends on highly volatile factors such as performance of the company, the industry and the market as a whole – and is thus highly volatile itself. Investors make lots of money – and lose lots, too – because of their decisions on which stocks to invest in, and what happened to the value of those stocks after they were bought.

The other component of the asset value of a company comes from its **debt**, which is represented by securities called bonds (these are issued when investors loan money to a company at a given interest rate). Typically, banks and large financial institutions invest in debt. The returns for debt investors are assured in the form of interest on the debt. Sometimes, the market value of the debt changes (see section on bond pricing), but bond prices usually do not change as drastically as stock prices can. On the downside, bonds also have lower expected returns than stocks. U.S. Treasury bonds, for example, can provide returns of 5 to 7% a year or so, while Yahoo! stock may rise 10% in a single day. On the other hand, bonds usually have less downside risk than stock. Though they won't post big gains, U.S. Treasury bonds won't lose 10% of their value in a single day, either.

A simple example of how debt and equity make up assets is to consider how most people buy homes. Homebuyers generally start with a down payment, which is a payment on the equity of the house. Then, the homebuyer makes mortgage payments that are a combination of debt (the interest on the mortgage) and equity (the principal payments). Initially, a homebuyer generally pays primarily interest (debt), before gradually buying larger and large portions of the principal (equity).

Preferred stock

Common stock and debt are the two extremes in the continuum of the forms of investment in a company. Enter preferred stock, which is a security in the middle of the continuum. One type of **preferred stock** is referred to as "convertible" preferred. If the preferred stock is convertible, it can be converted into common stock as prescribed in the initial issuance of the preferred stock. Like bondholders, holders of preferred stock are assured an interest-like return – also referred to as the preferred stock's "dividend." (A **dividend** is a payment made to stockholders, usually quarterly, that is intended to distribute some of the company's profits to shareholders.)

The other key difference between preferred and common stock comes into play when a company goes bankrupt. In what is referred to as the "seniority" of creditors, the debt holders have first claim on the assets of the firm if the company becomes insolvent. Preferred shareholders are next in line, while the common stock shareholders bring up the rear. This isn't just a matter of having to wait in line longer if you are a common stock shareholder. If the bondholders and owners of preferred stock have claims that exceed the value of the assets of a bankrupt company, the common stock shareholders won't see a dime.

There is a tax advantage for corporations to invest in preferred stock rather than in bonds for other companies. Corporate investors are taxed for only 30% of the dividends they receive on preferred stock. On the other hand, 100% of the interest payments on bonds paid to corporate investors are taxed. This tax rule comes in handy when structuring mergers.

Seniority of Creditors	
1.	Bondholders
2.	Preferred stockholders
3.	Common stockholders

Dividends

Dividends are paid to many shareholders of common stock (and preferred stock). However, the directors cannot pay any dividends to the common stock shareholders until they have paid all outstanding dividends to the preferred stockholders. The incentive for company directors to issue dividends is that companies in industries that are particularly "dividend sensitive" have better market valuations if they regularly issue dividends. Issuing regular dividends is a signal to the market that the company is doing well.

Unlike with bonds, however, the company directors decide when to pay the dividend on preferred stock. In contrast, if a company fails to meet a few bond payments as scheduled, the bondholders can force the company into Chapter 11 bankruptcy. (Bankruptcy filing in court come in two categories: Chapter 7 and Chapter 11. If a Chapter 7 bankruptcy filing is approved, the court puts a stay order on all interest payments — management is given a period of protection during which it can clean up its financial mess and try to get the house marching toward profitability. If the management fails to do so within the given time, there can be a Chapter 11 bankruptcy filing, when the assets of the company are liquidated.)

Stock splits

As a company grows in value, it usually splits its stock so that the price does not become absurdly high. This enables the company to maintain the liquidity of the stock. If The Coca-Cola Company had never split its stock, the price of one share bought when the company's stock was first offered would be worth millions of dollars. If that were the case, buying and selling one share would be a very crucial decision. This would adversely affect a stock's liquidity (that is, its ability to be freely traded on the market).

Stock buybacks

Often you will hear that a company has announced that it will buy back its own stock. Such an announcement is usually followed by an increase in the stock price. Why does a company buy back its stock? And why does its price increase after?

The reason behind the price increase is fairly complex, and involves three major reasons. The first has to do with the influence of earnings per share on market valuation. Many investors believe that if a company buys back shares, and the number of outstanding shares decreases, the company's earnings per share goes up. If the P/E (price to earnings-per-share ratio) stays stable, investors reason, the price should go up. Thus investors drive the stock price up in anticipation of increased earnings per share.

The second reason has to do with the "signaling effect." This reason is simple to understand, and largely explains why a company buys back stock. No one understands the health of the company better than its senior managers. No one is in a better position to judge what will happen to the future performance of the company. So if a company decides to buy back stock (i.e., decides to invest in its own stock), these managers must believe that the stock price is undervalued and will rise (or so most observers would believe). This is the signal company management sends to the market, and the market pushes the stock up in anticipation.

The other reason the stock price goes up after a buyback can be understood in terms of the "debt tax shield" (a concept used in valuation methods). When a company buys back stock, its net debt goes up (net debt = debt - cash). Thus the debt tax shield associated with the company goes up and the valuation rises (see APV valuation).

New stock issues

The reverse of a stock buyback is when a company issues new stock, which usually is followed by a drop in the company's stock price. As with stock buybacks, there are three main reasons for this movement. First, investors believe that issuing new shares "dilutes" earnings. That is, issuing new stock increases the number of outstanding shares, which decreases earnings per share, which — given a stable P/E ratio — decreases the share price. (Of course, the issuing of new stock will presumably be used in a way that will increase earnings, and thus the earnings per share figure won't necessarily decrease, but because investors believe in earnings dilution, they often drive stock prices down.)

There is also the signaling effect. In other words, investors may ask why the company's senior managers decided to issue equity rather than debt to meet their financing requirements. Surely, investors may believe, management must believe that the valuation of their stock is high (possibly inflated) and that by issuing stock they can take advantage of this high price.

Finally, if the company believes that the project for which they need money will definitely be successful, it would have issued debt, thus keeping all of the upside of the investment within the firm rather than distributing it away in the form of additional equity. The stock price also drops because of debt tax shield reasons. Because cash is flushed into the firm through the sale of equity, the net debt decreases. As net debt decreases, so does the associated debt tax shield.

Questions

1. What kind of stocks would you issue for a startup?

A startup typically has more risk than a well-established firm. The kind of stocks that one would issue for a startup would be those that protect the downside of equity holders while giving them upside. Hence the stock issued may be a combination of common stock, preferred stock and debt notes with warrants (options to buy stock).

2. When should a company buy back stock?

When it believes the stock is undervalued and believes it can make money by investing in itself. This can happen in a variety of situations. For example, if a company has suffered some decreased earnings because of an inherently cyclical industry (such as the semiconductor industry), and believes its stock price is unjustifiably low, it will buy back its own stock. On other occasions, a company will buy back its stock if investors are driving down the price precipitously. In this situation, the company is attempting to send a signal to the market that it is optimistic that its falling stock price is not justified. It's saying: "We know more than anyone else about our company. We are buying our stock back. Do you really think our stock price should be this low?"

3. Is the dividend paid on common stock taxable to shareholders? Preferred stock? Is it tax deductible for the company?

The dividend paid on common stock is taxable on two levels in the U.S. First at the firm level, as a dividend comes out from the net income after taxes (i.e., the money has been taxed once already) and then at the shareholder level. The shareholders are taxed for the dividend as ordinary income (O.I.). Dividend for preferred stock is treated as an interest expense and is tax-free at the corporate level.

4. When should a company issue stock rather than debt to fund its operations?

There are several reasons for a company to issue stock rather than debt. The first is if it believes its stock price is inflated, and it can raise money (on very good terms) by issuing stock. The second is when the projects for which the money is being raised may not generate predictable cash flows in the immediate future. A simple example of this is a startup company. The owners of startups generally will issue stock rather than take on debt because their ventures will probably not generate predictable cash flows, which is needed to make regular debt payments, and also so that the risk of the venture is diffused among the company's shareholders. A third reason for a company to raise money by selling equity is if it wants to change its debt-to-equity ratio. This ratio in part determines a company's bond rating. If a company's bond rating is poor because it is struggling with large debts, they may decide to issue equity to pay down the debt.

5. Why would an investor buy preferred stock?

(1.) An investor that wants the upside potential of equity but wants to minimize risk would buy preferred stock. The investor would receive steady interest-like payments (dividends) from the preferred stock that are more assured than the dividends from common stock. (2.) The preferred stock owner gets a superior right to the company's assets should the company go bankrupt. (3.) A corporation would invest in preferred stock because the dividends on preferred stock are taxed at a lower rate than the interest rates on bonds.

6. Why would a company distribute its earnings through dividends to common stockholders?

Regular dividend payments are signals that a company is healthy and profitable. Also, issuing dividends can attract investors (shareholders). Finally, a company may distribute earnings to shareholders if it lacks profitable investment opportunities.

7. What stocks do you like?

This is a question often asked of those applying for equity research positions. (Applicants for investment banking and trading positions, as well as investment management positions have also reported receiving this question.) If you're interviewing for one of these positions, you should prepare to talk about a couple of stocks you believe are good buys and some that you don't. This is also a question asked of undergraduate finance candidates to gauge their level of interest in finance.

8. What did the S&P 500 close at yesterday?

Another question designed to make sure that a candidate is sincerely interested in finance. This question (and others like it – "What's the Dow at now?" "What's the yield on the Long Bond?") can be expected especially of those looking for sales and trading positions.

9. Why did the stock price of XYZ company decrease yesterday when it announced increased quarterly earnings?

A couple of possible explanations: 1) the entire market was down, (or the sector to which XYZ belongs was down), or 2) even though XYZ announced increased earnings, the Street was expecting earnings to increase even higher.

10. Can you tell me about a recent IPO that you have followed?

Read the *Wall Street Journal* and stay current with recent offerings.

11. What is your investing strategy?

Different investors have different strategies. Some look for undervalued stocks, others for stocks with growth potential and yet others for stocks with steady performance. A strategy could also be focused on the long-term or short-term, and be more risky or less risky. Whatever your investing strategy is, you should be able to articulate these attributes.

12) How has your portfolio performed in the last five years?

If you are applying for an investment management firm as an MBA, you'd better have a good answer for this one. Also, if you think you are going to say it has outperformed the S&P each year, you better be well prepared to explain why you think this happened.

13) If you read that a given mutual fund has given 50% returns last year, would you invest in it?

You should look for more information, as past performance is not necessarily an indicator of future results. How has the overall market done? How did it do in the years before? Why did it give 50% returns last year? Can that strategy be expected to work continuously over the next five to 10 years? You need to look for answers to these questions before making a decision.

14) You are in the board of directors of a company and own a significant chunk of the company. The CEO, in his annual presentation states that the company's stock is doing as it has gone up 20% in the last 12 months. Is the company's stock doing well?

Another "trick" stock question that you should not answer too quickly. First, ask what the Beta of the company is. (Remember, the Beta represents the volatility of the stock with respect to the market.) If the Beta is 1 and the market (i.e. the Dow Jones Industrial Average) has gone up 35%, the company actually has not done too well in the stock market.

15) What is your Beta?

Don't be too surprised if an interviewer asks you this question. He/she could be doing this to throw you off guard! Take it in the spirit and reply based on how "risky" you think you are!

16. What do you think is happening with ABC stock?

Expect to be asked this question if you say you like to follow the Internet sector or the pharmaceutical sector. Interviewers will test you to see how well you know your industry. In case you don't know that stock, admit it, and offer to describe a stock in that sector that you like or have been following.

17. Where do you think the DJIA will be in three months and six months — and why?

Nobody knows the answer to this one. However, you should at least have some thoughts on the subject and be able to articulate why you think this is the case. If you have been following the performance of major macroeconomic indicators (which will be reviewed in the next section), you can state your case well.

18. Why do some stocks rise so much on the first day of trading and others don't? How is that "money left on the table?"

By "money left on the table," bankers mean that the company could have successfully completed the offering at a higher price, and that the difference in valuation thus goes to initial investors rather than the company. Why this happens and when it will happen is not easy to predict from responses received from investors during roadshows. Moreover, if the stock rises a lot the first day it is good publicity for the firm. But in many ways it is money left on the table because the company could have sold the same stock in its initial public offering at a higher price. However, bankers must honestly value a company and its stock over the long-term, rather than simply trying to guess what the market will do. Even if a stock trades up significantly initially, a banker looking at the long-term would expect the stock to come down, as long as the market eventually correctly values it.

19. What is insider trading and why is it illegal?

Undergraduates may get this question as feelers of their business knowledge. Insider trading describes the illegal activity of buying or selling stock based on information that is not public information. This is to prevent those with privileged information (company execs, I-bankers and lawyers) from using this information to make a tremendous amount of money unfairly.

20. Who is a more senior creditor, a bondholder or stockholder?

The bondholder is always more senior. Stockholders (including those who own preferred stock) must wait until bondholders are paid during a bankruptcy before claiming company assets.

Bonds & Interest Rates

What is a bond? A remedial lesson

A bond is a borrowing arrangement through which the borrower (or seller of a bond) issues or sells an IOU document to the investor (or buyer of the bond). The arrangement obligates the borrower to make specified payments to the bondholder on agreed-upon dates. For example, if you purchase a five-year U.S. Treasury note, the U.S. government is borrowing money from you for a period of five years. For this service, the government will pay you interest at the T-bill rate and return the amount it borrowed (called the principal) at the end of five years. Meanwhile, you can sell the bond in the market, too. Different types of organizations can issue bonds: companies like Ford Motor or Procter & Gamble, and municipal organizations, like counties and states.

Bond terminology

Before going any further in our discussion of bonds, we will introduce several terms you should be familiar with.

- **Par value or face value of a bond:** This is the total amount the bond issuer will commit to pay back at the end of the bond maturity period (when the bond expires).

- **Coupon payments:** The payments of interest that the bond issuer makes to the bondholder. These are often specified in terms of coupon rates. The coupon rate is the bond coupon payment divided by the bond's par value.

- **Bond price:** The price the bondholder (i.e. the lender) pays the bond issuer (i.e. the borrower) to hold the bond (to have a claim on the cash flows documented on the bond).

- **Default risk:** The risk that the company issuing the bond may go bankrupt, and "default" on its loans.

- **Default premium:** The difference between the promised yields on a corporate bond and the yield on an otherwise identical government bond. In theory, the difference compensates the bondholder for the corporation's default risk.

- **Credit ratings:** Bonds are rated by credit agencies (Moody's, Standard & Poor's), which examine a company's financial situation, outstanding debt, and other factors to determine the risk of default. Companies guard their credit ratings closely, because with high ratings, they can raise money easily at lower interest rates.

- **Investment grade bonds:** These bonds have high credit ratings, and pay a relatively low rate of interest.

- **Junk bonds:** Also known as "high yield bonds," these bonds have poor credit ratings, and pay a relatively high rate of interest.
- **U.S. Treasury bills, notes, and bonds:** "Bills" mature in one year or less, "notes" in two to 10 years., and "bonds" in 30 years. (The 30-year U.S. Treasury bond is also called **The Long Bond**.")

How a bond works

To illustrate how a bond works, let's look at an 8% coupon, 30-year maturity bond with a par value of $1,000, paying 60 coupon payments of $40 each.

Let's illustrate this bond with the following schematic:

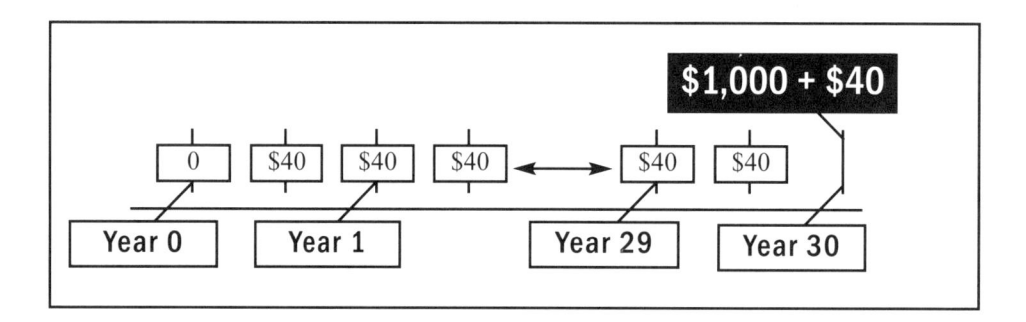

```
     0    $40   $40   $40  ←→  $40   $40   $1,000 + $40
   Year 0  Year 1           Year 29  Year 30
```

Coupon rate = 8%

Par value = $1,000

Therefore the coupon = 8% x $1,000 = $80 per year

Since this bond is a semiannual coupon, the payments are for $40 every six months. We can also say that the semiannual coupon rate is 4%.

Since its time to maturity is 30 years, there are total of 30 x 2 = 60 semiannual payments.

At the end of Year 30, the bondholder receives the last semiannual payment of $40 dollars plus the principal of $1,000.

Pricing bonds

The question now is how much such a bond is worth?

The price of a bond is the net present value of all future cash flows expected from that bond. (Recall net present value from our discussion on valuation.)

$$\text{Bond Value} = \sum_{t=1}^{T}\left(\frac{\text{Coupon}}{(1+r)^t}\right) + \frac{\text{Par Value}}{(1+r)^T}$$

Where:

r = Discount rate

t = Interval (for example, 6 months)

T = Total payments

First, we must ask what discount rate should be used? Remember from our discussion of valuation techniques that discount rate for a cash flow for a given period should be able to account for the risk associated with the cash flow for that period. In practice, there will be different discount rates for cash flows occurring in different periods. However, for the sake of simplicity, we will assume that the discount rate is the same as the interest rate on the bond.

So, what is the price of the bond described earlier? From the equation above we get:

$$\text{Price} = \sum_{t=1}^{T}\left(\frac{\$40}{(1+.04)^t}\right) + \frac{\$1000}{(1+.04)^{60}}$$

Calculating the answer for this equation is complex. Luckily, this can be solved using a financial calculator. Also, there are Present Value tables available that simplify the calculations. In this case, the % is 4 % and T is 60. Using the Present Value tables we get

= $757.17 + $53.54

= $810.71

Also, if we look at the bond price equation closely, we see that the bond price depends on the interest rate. *If the interest rate is higher, the bond price is lower and vice versa.* This is a fundamental rule that should be understood and remembered.

Other bond concepts

The Yield to Maturity (YTM)

The measure of the average rate of return that will be earned on a bond if it is bought now and held until maturity. To calculate this, we need the information on bond price, coupon rate and par value of the bond.

Example: Suppose an 8% coupon, 30-year bond is selling at $1,276.76. What average rate of return would be earned if you purchase the bond at this price?

To answer this question, we must find the interest rate at which the present value of the bond payments equals the bond price. This is the rate that is consistent with the observed price of the bond. Therefore, we solve for r in the following equation.

$$\$1276.76 = \sum_{t=1}^{60} \left(\frac{\$40}{(1+r)^t} \right) + \frac{\$1,000}{(1+r)^{60}}$$

This equation can be solved using a financial calculator; in completing the calculation we see that the bond's yield to maturity is 3%.

Holding Period Return (HPR)

The income earned over a period as a percentage of the bond price at the start of the period, assuming that the bond is sold at the end of the period.

Example: Let's take a 30-year bond, with an $80 coupon, purchased for $1000 with a Yield to Maturity (YTM) of 8%. Say at the end of the year, the bond price increases to $1,050. Then the YTM will go below 8%, but the HPR will be higher than 8% and is given by:

$$HPR = \frac{(\$80) + (\$1,050 - \$1,000)}{\$1,000} = 13\%$$

Callable Bonds

For the sake of simplification in our earlier discussions, we assumed that the discount rate was equal to the interest rate, and that the interest rate was constant at the coupon rate. However, in the real world, this is not always the case.

If the interest rate falls, bond prices can rise substantially.

We'll explain why this happens with an example. Let's say a company has a bond outstanding. It took $810.71 and promised to make the coupon payments as described above, at $40 every six months. Let's say the market interest rates dropped after a while (below 8%). According to the bond document, the company is still expected to pay the coupon at a rate of 8%.

If the interest rates were to drop in this manner, the company would be paying a coupon rate much higher than the market interest rate today. In such a situation, the company may want to buy the bond back so that it is not committed to paying large coupon payments in the future. This is referred to as "**calling the bond**." However, an issuer can only "call" a bond if the bond was originally issued as a callable bond. The risk that a bond will be called is reflected in the bond's price. The yield calculated up to the period when the bond is called back is referred to as the **yield to call.**

Zero Coupon Bonds
This type of bond offers no coupon or interest payments to the bondholder. The only payment the zero coupon bondholder receives is the payment of the bond face value upon maturity. The returns on a coupon bonds must be obtained through price appreciation. These bonds are priced at a considerable discount to par value.

Forward Rates
These are agreed-upon interest rates for a bond to be issued in the future. For example, the one year forward rate for a five-year U.S. Treasury note represents the interest "forward" rate on a five-year T-note that will be issued one year from now (and that will mature six years from now). This "forward" rate changes daily just like the rates of already-issued bonds. It is essentially based on the market's expectation of what the interest rate a year from now will be, and can be calculated using the rates of current bonds.

The Fed and interest rates

The Federal Reserve Board has the broad responsibility for the health of the U.S. financial system. In this role, the Fed sets the margin requirements on stocks and options, and regulates bank lending to securities market participants.

The Fed also has the responsibility of formulating the nation's monetary policy. In determining the monetary policy of the nation, the Fed manipulates the money supply to effect the macroeconomy. When the Fed increases the money supply to the economy, the monetary policy set by the Fed is said to be **expansionary.**" This encourages investment and subsequently increases consumption demand. In the long run, however, an expansionary policy can lead to higher prices and inflation. Therefore, it is the Fed's responsibility to maintain a proper balance and prevent the economy from either hyperinflation or recession.

The Fed uses several tools to regulate the money supply. The Fed can 1) use its "check writing capabilities" (2 raise or lower the interest rates, or 3) manipulate the reserve requirements for various banks to control the money flow and thereby the interest rate.

Let's look at these one by one:

1. **Open Market Operations**

   The Fed can "write a check" to buy securities and thereby increase the money supply. Unlike the rest of us, the Fed doesn't have to pay the money for a check it has written. As we will see, an increase in the country's money supply stimulates the economy. Likewise, if the Fed sells securities, the money paid for them leaves the money supply and slows the economy.

2. **Changing Interest Rates**

   The Fed can raise or lower interest rates by changing: (a) the discount rate (the interest rate the Fed charges banks on short-term loans), and/or (b) the Federal Funds rate (or "Fed Funds" rate), (the rate banks charge each other on short-term loans). When the Fed raises or lowers interest rates, banks usually quickly follow by raising or lowering their "prime rate" (the rate banks charge on loans to its most creditworthy customers). A reduction of the interest rate signals an expansionary monetary policy. Why? Because by reducing the interest of its loans to banks, the Fed allows banks to lend out money at lower rates. More businesses and individuals are willing to take out loans, thus pouring more money into the economy.

3. **Reserve Requirements**

   All banks that are members of the Federal Reserve System are required to maintain a minimum balance in a reserve account with the Fed. The amount of this minimum balance depends on the total deposits of the bank's customers. These minimum deposits are referred to as "reserve requirements." Lowering the reserve requirements for various banks has the same expansionary effect. This move allows banks to make more loans with the deposits it has and thereby stimulates the economy by increasing the money supply.

But why does an increase in money supply stimulate the economy? An increase in the money supply usually results in investors having too much money in their portfolios, which leads them to buy more bonds. This increases the demand for bonds, drives up bond prices, and thereby reduces interest rates. More money available increases demand for stocks and subsequently real estate. This leads to higher investments and greater demand for goods.

The Fed and inflation

Inflation is the rise of prices over time — it is why over the long-term, we are guaranteed to hear and (sorry, it's true) speak phrases like: "When I was your age, a can of Coke was only 50 cents."

Inflation directly affects interest rates. Consider this: If lending money is healthy for the economy because it promotes growth, interest rates must be higher than inflation. (If I lent out money at a 5 percent annual interest rate, but inflation was at 10 percent, I would never lend money.) Thus, the Federal Reserve watches inflation closely in its role of setting interest rates. Moreover, lenders issuing long-term loans such as mortgages can issue what are called "**floating rate**" loans, whose yield depends on an interest rate (like the prime rate) that adjusts to account for changes in inflation. In this way, lenders can be protected should inflation increase.

At the same time, some amount of inflation (usually around 1 to 2 percent) is a sign of a healthy economy. If the economy is healthy and the stock market is growing, consumer spending increases. This means that people are buying more goods, and by consequence, more goods are in demand. No inflation means that you do not have a robust economy — that there is no competitive demand for goods.

But "**good inflation**" must be watched closely. From basic microeconomics we know that if the demand curve shifts upwards because of higher income, the new equilibrium price is higher. Once the price rises, the supply curve shifts as more people (sellers) enter the market to take advantage of the opportunity (i.e. growth in macroeconomic terms). This causes the supply curve to also shift upwards — the prices reach a new equilibrium above the previous equilibrium. As you can see, this can theoretically spiral upward, as increased supply indicating a healthy economy further boosts the demand and so on. This is Federal Reserve Chairman Alan Greenspan's major concern with an "irrationally exuberant" stock market — that the economy will overheat as a result and inflation will spiral out of control.

Effect of inflation on bond prices

The rule is very simple: when inflation goes up, interest rates rise. And when interest rates raise bond prices fall. Therefore, when inflation goes up, bond prices fall.

The ways in which economic events, inflation, interest rates, and bond prices interact are the basics of an understanding of finance — these relationships are sure to be tested in finance interviews. In general, a positive economic event (such as a decrease in unemployment, greater consumer confidence, higher personal income, etc.) drives up inflation (because there are more people working, there is more money to be spent), which drives up interest rates, which causes a decrease in bond prices (although the yield on bonds increases).

The following table summarizes this relationship with a variety of economic events.

Economic Event	Inflation	Interest Rates	Bond Prices
Unemployment figures low	Up	Up	Down
Dollar weakens against Yen	Up	Up	Down
Consumer confidence low	Down	Down	Up
Stock Market drops	Down	Down	Up
Companies report healthy earnings	Up	Up	Down

Leading Economic Indicators

The following table is a look at leading economic indicators, and whether their rise or fall signal positive economic events or negative economic events. For finance interviews, know this chart cold!

Indicator	Positive Economic Event	Negative Economic Event
GDP	Up	Down
Unemployment	Down	Up
Inflation	Down	Up
Consumer Price Index	Down	Up
Interest Rate	Down	Up
New Home Starts	Up	Down
Existing Home Sales	Up	Down

Questions

1. How are bonds priced?

Bonds are priced based on the net present value of all future cash flows expected from the bond.

2. How would you value a perpetual bond that pays you $1,000 a year in coupons?

Divide the coupon by the current interest rate. For example, a corporate bond with an interest rate of 10% that pays $1,000 a year in coupons would be worth $10,000.

3. When should a company issue debt instead of issuing equity?

First, a company needs a steady cash flow before it can consider issuing debt (otherwise, it can quickly fall behind interest payments and eventually see its assets seized). Once a company can issue debt, it will do so for a couple of main reasons.

If the expected return on equity is higher than the expected return on debt, a company will issue debt. For example, say a company believes that projects completed with the $1 million raised through either an equity or debt offering will increase its market value from $4 million to $10 million. It also knows that the same amount could be raised by issuing a $1 million bond that requires $300,000 in interest payments over its life. If the company issues equity, it will have to sell 20% of the company ($1 million / $4 million). This would then grow to 20% of $10 million, or $2 million. Thus, issuing the equity will cost the company $1 million ($2 million - $1 million). The debt, on the other hand, will only cost $300,000. The company will therefore choose to issue debt in this case, as the debt is "cheaper" than the equity.

Also, interest payments on bonds are tax deductible. A company may also wish to issue debt if it has taxable income and can benefit from tax shields.

4. What major factors affect the yield on a corporate bond?

The short answer: (1) interest rates on comparable U.S. Treasury bonds, and (2) the company's credit risk. A more elaborate answer would include a discussion of the fact that corporate bond yields trade at a premium, or "spread," over the interest rate on comparable U.S. Treasury bonds. (For example, a five-year corporate bond that trades at a premium of ½%, or "50 basis points," over the five-year Treasury note is priced at "50 over.") How large this "spread" is depends on the company's credit risk: the riskier the company, the higher the interest rate the company must pay to convince investors to lend it money and, therefore, the wider the spread over U.S. Treasuries.

5. If you believe interest rates will fall, which should you buy: a 10-year coupon bond or a 10-year zero coupon bond?

The 10-year zero coupon bond. A zero coupon bond is more sensitive to changes in interest rates than an equivalent coupon bond, so its price will increase more if interest rates fall.

6. Which is riskier: a 30-year coupon bond or a 30-year zero coupon bond?

A 30-year zero coupon bond. Here's why: A coupon bond pays interest semi-annually, then pays the principal when the bond matures (after 30 years, in this case). A zero coupon bond pays no interest, but pays one lump sum upon maturity (after 30 years, in this case). The coupon bond is less risky because you receive some of your money back before over time, whereas with a zero coupon bond you must wait 30 years to receive any money back. (Another answer: The zero coupon bond is more risky because its price is more sensitive to changes in interest rates.)

7. What is The Long Bond trading at?

The Long Bond is the U.S. Treasury's 30-year bond. In particular for sales & trading positions, but also for corporate finance positions, interviewers want to see that you're interested in the financial markets and follow them daily.

Vault.com Guide to Finance Interviews

Bonds & Interest Rates

8. If the price of the 10-year Treasury note rises, does the note's yield rise, fall or stay the same?

Bond yields move in the opposite direction of bond prices. Therefore, if the price of a 10-year note rises, its yield will fall.

9. If you believe interest rates will fall, should you buy bonds or sell bonds?

Since bond prices rise when interest rates fall, you should buy bonds.

10. How many "basis points" equal ½ percent?

Bond yields are measured in "basis points," which are $1/100$ of 1%. 1% = 100 basis points. Therefore, ½ percent = 50 basis points.

11. Why can inflation hurt creditors?

Think of it this way: If you are a creditor lending out money at a fixed rate, inflation cuts into the percentage that you are actually making. If you lend out money at 7% a year, and inflation is 5%, you are only really clearing 2%.

12. How would the following affect the interest rates? U.S. bombers attack Iraq (again). The President is impeached and convicted.

While it can't be said for certain, chances are that these kind of events will lead to fears that the economy will go into recession, so the Fed would want to balance that by giving expansionary signals and lowering interest rates.

13. What does the government do when there is a fear of hyperinflation?

The government has fiscal and monetary policies it can use in order to control hyperinflation. The monetary policies (the Fed's use of interest rates, reserve requirements, etc.) are discussed in detail in this chapter. The fiscal policies include the use of taxation and government spending to regulate the aggregate level of economic activity. Increasing taxes and decreasing government spending slows down growth in the economy and fights inflationary fears.

14. Where do you think the U.S. economy will go over the next year?

Talking about the U.S. economy encompasses a lot of topics: the stock market, consumer spending, unemployment, etc. Underlying all these topics are the way interest rates, inflation, and bonds interact. Make sure you can speak articulately about the concepts discussed in this chapter as they relate to the current situation.

15. How would you value a perpetual zero coupon bond?

The value will be zero. A zero coupon doesn't pay any coupons, and if that continues on perpetually, when do you get paid? Never — so it ain't worth nothing!

16. Let's say a report released today showed that inflation last month was very low. However, bond prices closed lower. Why might this happen?

Bond prices are based on expectations of future inflation. In this case, you can assume that traders expect future inflation to be higher (regardless of the report on last month's inflation figures) and therefore they bid bond prices down today. (A report which showed that inflation last month was benign would benefit bond prices only to the extent that traders believed it was an indication of low future inflation as well.)

Bonds & Interest Rates

17. If the stock market falls, what would you expect to happen to bond prices, and interest rates?

Bond prices increase and interest rates fall.

18. If unemployment is low, what happens to inflation, interest rates, and bond prices?

Inflation goes up, interest rates also increase, and bond prices decrease.

Currencies

In this global economy, an understanding of how currencies interact and what influences currency rates is vital for those interested in finance careers. The strength and stability of currencies influence trade and foreign investment. Why did so many U.S. investment banks suffer when Asian currencies plummeted in recent years? What does a "strong" dollar mean? When a company makes foreign investments or does business in foreign countries, how is it affected by the exchange rates among currencies? These are all issues that you'll need to know as you advance in your finance career.

To begin our discussion of currencies, let's look at some of the major terms used to discuss currencies:

Spot Exchange Rate: The prices of currencies for immediate delivery. (The "exchange rate" people commonly talk about is actually the spot exchange rate.)

Example: Let's say that today the spot rate of U.S. dollars to the British pound is $1.5628/£1. If you go to the bank today, and present a teller with $1,562.80, you will receive £1,000.

Forward Exchange Rate: The prices of currencies at which they can be bought and sold for future delivery.

Example: Let's say that today the one-month forward rate for British pound is $1.5629, the three-month rate is $1.5625, and the one-year rate is $1.5619. These represent the prices at which the market (buyers and sellers) would agree (today) to exchange currencies one month, three months, or a year from now.

In this example, the dollar is said to be trading at a one-month **forward discount**, because you can get fewer pounds for the dollar in the future than you can today. Alternately, the dollar is trading at a **forward premium** for a three-month or a year period, because you can get more pounds for the dollar in the future than you can today.

Exchange rates

So what determines the rate at which dollars and pounds, or dollars and baht, or baht and roubles are exchanged? The perfect market exchange rate between two currencies is determined primarily by two factors: the interest rates in the two countries and the rates of inflation in the two countries. However, in the real world, governments of many countries regulate the exchange rate to control growth and investment of foreign capital in the economy. Economists believe that such artificial controls are the main reason currencies fall so drastically sometimes (such as the 1997-98 collapse of the Russian rouble and many Asian currencies).

Strong/Weak Currencies: When a currency is "**strong**," that means its value is rising relative to other currencies. This is also called "**currency appreciation**." When a currency is weak, its value is falling relative to other currencies. This is also called "**currency depreciation**."

Example: Let's say the dollar-pound exchange rate on January 1 is $1.50/£1. Three months later, on March 1, the exchange rate is $1.60/£1. The dollar has "weakened," or "depreciated" against the pound, because it takes more dollars to equal 1 pound.

Influence of interest rates on foreign exchange

The foreign exchange rate between two currencies is related to the interest rates in the two countries. If the interest rate of a foreign country relative to the home country goes up, the home currency weakens. In other words, it takes more of the home currency to buy the same amount of foreign currency. (Note: We are talking here about the "real" interest rate, or the interest rate after inflation. After all, if interests rates and inflation were to go up by the same amount, the effect on the country's currency would generally be a "wash," of no net effect.)

Example: Let's say the risk-free interest rate in the U.S. is 5%; and in the U.K. it is 10%. Let's also assume that the exchange rate today is $1.5/£1. If the U.K. interest rate rises to 12%, the British pound will tend to strengthen against the dollar.

Explanation: When interest rates in a country rise, investments held in that country's currency (for example, bank deposits, bonds, CDs, etc.) will earn a higher rate of return. Therefore, when a country's interest rates rise, money and investments will tend to flow to that country, driving up the value of its currency. (The reverse is true when a country's interest rates fall.)

Influence of inflation on foreign exchange

If the inflation in the foreign country goes up relative to the home currency, the foreign currency devalues or "weakens" relative to the home currency. In other words, it takes less of the home currency to buy the same amount of foreign currency.

Example: Let us say that at the beginning of the year, silver costs $1,500/lb in the U.S. and £1,000/lb in the U.K. At the same time it takes $1.5 to buy £1. Let us now assume that inflation in the U.K. is at 10% while that in the U.S. is at 0%. At the end of the year, the silver still costs $1,500/lb in the U.S., but it costs pounds £1,100 in U.K. because of inflation. Because of the U.K.'s higher inflation rate, the British pound will weaken relative to the dollar (so that, for example, it may take $1.60 to buy £1).

Advanced Explanation: Let's say again that at the beginning of the year, silver costs $1,500/lb in the U.S. and £1,000/lb in the U.K. At the same time, it takes $1.5 to buy £1. Let us now assume that inflation in the U.K. is at 10% while inflation in the U.S. is at 0%.

At the end of the year, the silver still costs $1,500/lb in the U.S., but it costs £1,100/lb in U.K. because of inflation. If the exchange rate were to remain the same, people would start buying silver in the U.S., selling it in the U.K., and converting their money back to dollars, thus making a tidy profit. In other words, if you had $1,500, you would buy a pound of silver in U.S., sell it in U.K. for £1,100 at the end of the year, convert the

British pounds into dollars at $1.5/£1, thus receiving $1,650. For each pound of silver with which you did this, you would make a neat profit of $150. If you were to do that with a billion dollars worth of silver, you could pay for the travel expenses and buy homes in London and New York. I have been able to take advantage of the inflation in the U.K. and created an arbitrage opportunity.

In the real world, this does not happen. If there is inflation in the U.K., the value of the pound will weaken. This is given by the relationship below.

$$\frac{f\$/£}{s\$/£} = \frac{(1 + i\$)}{(1 + i£)}$$

Here:

i$ = the inflation in $ and

i£ = the inflation in £

Capital market equilibrium

The principle of **capital market equilibrium** (CME) states that there should be equilibrium in the interest rate markets all over the world so that there is no arbitrage opportunity in shifting between two currencies. For example, if you could buy 1 pound for every 1.5 dollars, and 60 Indian Rupees for every pound, you should only be able to by a dollar for every 40 Rupees.

$$\frac{Rs60}{£1} \times \frac{£1}{\$1.5} = \frac{Rs40}{\$1}$$

Consider what would happen if this was not the case? Say the dollar/pound exchange rate was $2/£1 instead of $1.5/£1, but the Rupee/dollar and Rupee/pound relationships remained the same (1$/40 Rs and £1/60 Rs)? You could take $100, convert it into 4,000 rupees, take those rupees and convert it into pounds 66.67, and finally, take those 66.67 pounds and convert that back into $133.3. You could sit at home and churn out millions of dollars this way!

Step 1: Convert dollars to rupees $\quad \$100 \times \frac{Rs40}{\$1} = 4,000 \text{ Rs}$

Step 2: Convert rupees to pounds $\quad 4,000 \text{ Rs} \times \frac{£1}{60 \text{ Rs}} = £66.67$

Step 3: Convert pounds to dollars $\quad £66.67 \times \frac{\$2}{£1} = \$133.33$

The three factors

These three factors — interest rates, inflation, and the principle of capital market equilibrium – govern the valuation of various currencies relative to each other. Because the U.S. dollar is generally considered the world's most stable currency, it is the widely accepted standard for foreign exchange valuation. Other currencies that are considered stable are the Japanese yen and the German deutsch mark. The relative movements of these currencies, as well as others, are monitored daily.

Effect of exchange rates on earnings of companies

Companies that do business abroad are exposed to currency risk. For example, if a U.S. company that manufactures goods in the U.S. sells them in England, its quarterly earnings will fluctuate based on fluctuating dollar-pound exchange rates.

If the dollar weakens, (i.e. one dollar can buy fewer pounds), the company's earnings will increase because when the pounds earned by selling the product are sent back to the U.S., they will be able to buy more dollars. If the dollar strengthens, then the earnings will go down. It is important to note that there are several complex accounting rules that govern how these earnings are accounted for. Let's look at another example.

Example: *If Coca-Cola sells soda in the U.K. for £1 per 2-liter bottle, and the dollar-pound exchange rate is $1.50/£1, Coca-Cola really gets $1.50 per 2-liter bottle it sells in England. If the dollar weakens, so that the exchange rate is $1.60/£1, Coca-Cola will in fact get $1.60 per pound and its earnings will be positively impacted (all else being equal).*

The following table summarizes the effect of exchange rates on multinational companies.

Economic Event	Effect on Earnings of U.S. Multi-National Companies	Inflation	Interest Rates
U.S. Dollar Strengthens	Negative	Falls	Fall
U.S. Dollar Weakens	Positive	Rises	Rise

Effect of exchange rates on interest rates and inflation

A weak dollar means that the prices of imported goods will rise when measured in U.S. dollars (i.e., it will take more dollars to buy the same good). When the prices of imported goods rise, this contributes to higher inflation, which also raises interest rates. Conversely, a strong dollar means that the prices of imported goods will fall, which will lower inflation (which will lower interest rates). The following table summarizes the relationship between interest rates, inflation, and exchange rates.

Economic Event	Effect on Dollar
U.S. (Real) Interest Rates Rise	Strengthens
U.S. (Real) Interest Rates Fall	Weakens
U.S. Inflation Rates Rise	Weakens
U.S. Inflation Rates Fall	Strengthens

Currency devaluation and revaluation

Under a fixed-exchange-rate system, in which exchange rates are changed only by official government action, different terms are used. Instead of depreciation, a weakening of the currency is called "**devaluation**." To take a recent example, devaluation is what occurred in Indonesia in 1998. The Indonesian government had pegged its currency, the rupiah, to the American dollar in an attempt to artificially maintain its strength. As this policy became untenable, the government devalued its currency, causing foreign investment to flee the country and throwing the country's economy into turmoil. A strengthening of the currency under fixed exchange rates is called "**revaluation**," rather than appreciation. These terms can be summarized in the following chart.

Type of exchange rate system	Home currency strengthens	Home currency weakens
Flexible	Appreciation	Depreciation
Fixed	Revaluation	Devaluation

Questions

1. What is the currency risk for a company like Microsoft? What about Ford?

Microsoft and Ford have different currency risks. Let's take Microsoft first. Its currency risks are created by its sales in foreign countries. For example, if it markets a software program for 100 RMB in China, and the dollar strengthens against the RMB (and the company doesn't change its price), Microsoft will be making less in U.S. dollars than it had previously anticipated. Of course, it can react by changing its prices.

Now let's examine Ford's currency risks. Like Microsoft, Ford is vulnerable to currency risks because it sells products in foreign currencies. In addition, the auto giant is vulnerable because it manufactures cars overseas. Let's say the company has manufacturing operations in Mexico, where cars are built, later be sold in the U.S. The cost of those operations will be sensitive to the price of the peso relative to the dollar. If the peso weakens, Ford can make its cars cheaper, sell them for lower prices, and thus gain a competitive advantage. But the opposite is also true. If the peso strengthens, Ford's labor costs will shoot up. In contrast, Microsoft doesn't have manufacturing costs overseas (most of its production costs are spent in Redmond rather than at cheaper production facilities overseas). Ford's currency risk is further complicated because some of its major competitors are in countries outside the U.S. For example, the price of the deutsch mark and the yen influences the prices at which German and Japanese competitors sell their cars. Thus Ford has greater currency risk than Microsoft.

2. When the currencies in companies like Thailand, Indonesia, and Russia fell drastically recently, why were U.S. and European-based investment banks hurt so badly?

I-banks were hurt on trading losses in Asia and Russia. If banks held either currency or bonds in the currencies that dropped, these assets suddenly turned "non-performing," in other words, essentially worthless. (In fact, Russia's government defaulted on its government-backed bonds, so firms weren't just hurt by dropping currencies but also by loan defaults.)

Vault.com Guide to Finance Interviews
Currencies

3. If the U.S. dollar weakens, should interest rates generally rise, fall or stay the same?

Rise. A weak dollar means that the prices of imported goods will rise when measured in U.S. dollars (i.e., it will take more dollars to buy the same good). When the prices of imported goods rise, this contributes to higher inflation, which raises interest rates.

4. If U.S. inflation rates fall, what will happen to the dollar?

It will strengthen.

5. If the interest rate in Brazil increases relative to that in the U.S., what will happen to the exchange rate between the real and the dollar?

The real will strengthen relative to the dollar.

6. If inflation rates in the U.S. falls relative to the inflation rate in Russia, what will happen to the exchange rate between the dollar and the rouble?

The dollar will strengthen relative to the rouble.

7. What is the difference between currency devaluation and currency depreciation?

Devaluation occurs in a fixed-exchange-rate system, while depreciation occurs when a country allows its currency to move according to the international currency exchange market.

8. What is the effect on U.S. multinational companies if the U.S. dollar strengthens?

U.S. multinationals see their earnings decrease when the dollar strengthens. Why? Essentially, the sales in foreign currencies don't amount to as many U.S. dollars when the dollar strengthens.

9. What factors govern foreign exchange rates?

Chiefly: interest rates, inflation, and capital market equilibrium.

10. If the spot exchange rate of dollars to pounds is $1.60/£1, and the one-year forward rate is $1.50/£1, would we say the dollar is strong or weak relative to the pound?

The forward exchange rate indicates the rate at which traders are willing to exchange currencies in the future. In this case, they believe that the dollar will strengthen against the pound in the coming year (that one dollar will be able to buy more pounds one year from now than it can now).

Options & Derivatives

Derivatives aren't the most trusted of financial instruments. They received some bad press in the mid-1990s when Bankers Trust, the leading marketer of derivatives, was accused by several of its key clients, including Procter & Gamble and Gibson Greetings, of misinforming them about the riskiness of its derivatives instruments. The trustworthiness of derivatives wasn't helped any when Bankers Trust bankers, who had a reputation for being high-flying risk-takers, were caught on tape making dismissive comments about whether their clients would be able to understand what they were doing or had done wrong. Derivatives received another black mark for their role in the bankruptcy of Orange County, California, the largest municipal bankruptcy in U.S. history. In a case similar to the Bankers Trust case, Orange County officials charged that they had been misled about the riskiness of their investments, which involved complex derivatives. To settle that suit, the county's lead investment banker, Merrill Lynch, agreed to pay $437.1 million.

What are these scary things called derivatives? Quite simply, derivatives are financial instruments that derive their value out of or have their value contingent on the values of other assets like stocks, bonds, commodity prices or market index values.

Derivatives are often used to "hedge" financial positions. Hedging is a financial strategy designed to reduce risk by balancing a position in the market. Often, hedges work like insurance: a small position pays off large amounts if the price of a certain security reaches a certain price. On other occasions, derivatives are used to hedge positions by locking in prices.

Options

We'll begin our discussion of derivatives with a look at options, the most common form of derivatives. Options, as the word suggests, give the bearers the right to buy or sell a security — without the obligation to do so. Two of the simplest forms of options are "call" options and "put" options.

Call options

A "**call option**" gives the holder the right to purchase an asset for a specified price on or before a specified expiration date. (This specified price is called the "exercise price" or "strike price.") Let's take a look at an example — a July 1 call option on IBM stock with an exercise price of $70. The owner of this option is entitled to purchase IBM stock at $70 at anytime up to and including the expiration date of July 1. If in June, the price of IBM stock jumps up to $80, the holder can exercise the option to buy stock from the option seller for $70. The holder can then turn around and sell it to the market for $80 and make a neat profit of $10 per share (minus the price of the option, which we will discuss later).

Note: When a call option's exercise price is exactly equal to the current stock price, the option is called an "**at the money**" call. When a call option whose exercise price is less than the current stock price, it is called an "**in the money**" call. When a call option's exercise price is greater than the current stock price, it is called an "**out of the money**" call.

Put options

The other common form of option is a "**put option**." A put option gives its holder the right to sell an asset for a specified exercise price on or before a specified expiration date. For example, a July 1 put option on IBM with an exercise price of $70 entitles its owner to sell IBM stock at $70 at any time before it expires in July, even if market price is lower than $70. So if the price drops to $60, the holder of the put option would buy the stock at $60, sell it for $70 by exercising her option, and make a neat profit of $10 (minus the price of the option). On the other hand, if the price goes over $70, the holder of the put option will not exercise the option and will lose the amount he paid to buy the option.

Writing options

Sounds pretty neat, eh? But how are these options created? And who buys and sells the stock that the options give holders the right to buy and sell?

Well, there is an entire market — called the options market — that helps these transactions go through. For every option holder there must be an option seller. This seller is often referred to as the "writer" of the option. So selling a put option is called "writing a put." Anyone who owns the underlying asset, such as an individual or a mutual fund — can write options.

Let's go back to our previous example. If you buy the July 1 call option on IBM stock with an exercise price of $70, you are betting that the price of IBM will go above $70 before July 1. You can make this bet only if there is someone who believes that the price of IBM will not go above $70 before July 1. That person is the seller, or writer, of the call option. If the price goes to $80 in June and you exercise your option, the person who sold the call option has to buy the stock from the market at $80 (assuming he does not already own it) and sell it to you at $70, thus incurring a loss of $10.

But remember that you had to buy the option originally. The seller of the option, who has just incurred a loss of $10, already received the price of the option when you bought the option. On the other hand, say the price had stayed below $70 and closed at $60 on June 30. The seller would have made the amount he sold the option for, but would not make the difference between the $70 strike price and the $60 June 30 closing price. Why not? Because as the buyer of the call option, you have the right to buy at $70 but is not obligated to. If the stock price of IBM stays below $70, you as the option buyer will not exercise the option.

Note: If the writer of the call option already owns IBM stock, he is essentially "selling you his upside" on his IBM stock, or the right to all gains above $70. Obviously, he doesn't think it's very likely that IBM will rise above $70 and he hopes to simply pocket the option price.

Summary options chart

	Action to take
Person believes a stock will go up	Buy a call
	Write a put
Person believes a stock will go down	Buy a put
	Write a call

Options pricing

Understanding how an option writer makes money brings up the natural question: How does an option get priced?

There are at least six factors that affect the value of an option: the stock price, exercise price, the volatility of the stock price, the time to expiration, the interest rate and the dividend rate of the stock. To understand how these factors affect option values, we will look at their effect on call options (the option to buy a security).

- <u>Price of underlying security</u>. If an option is purchased at a fixed exercise price, and the price of the underlying stock increases, the value of a call option increases. Clearly, if you have the option to buy IBM stock at $100, the value of your option will increase with any increase in stock price: from $95 to $100, from $100 to $105, from $105 to $106, etc. (The value of a put option in this scenario decreases.)

- Exercise ("strike") price. Call options can be bought at various exercise prices. For example, you can buy an option to buy stock in IBM at $100, or you can buy an option to buy stock in IBM at $110. The higher the exercise price, the lower the value of the call option, as the stock price has to go up higher for you to be in the money.. (Here, the value of the put option increases, as the stock price does not need to fall as low.)

- Volatility of underlying security. The option value increases if the volatility of the underlying stock increases. Let's compare similar options on a volatile Internet stock like eBay and a more steady stock like Wal-Mart. Say that the eBay stock price has been fluctuating from $70 to $130 in the last three months. Let's also say that Wal-Mart has been fluctuating from $90 to $110. Now let's compare call options with an exercise price of $100 and a time until expiration of three months. Although the average price for both stocks in the past three months has been $100, you would value the option to buy eBay stock more because there is a greater possibility that it will increase well above $100. (Perhaps eBay would rise to $130, rather than Wal-Mart's $110, if the previous three months were replicated.) The reason this potential upside increases the option's value is that the downside loss that you can incur is fixed! You have the "option" to exercise and not the obligation to buy at $100. No matter how low eBay's stock might go, the most you would lose is the cost of the option. Volatility increases the value of both call and put options.

- Time to expiration. The more time the holder has to exercise the option, the more valuable the option. This makes common sense. The further away the exercise date, there is more time for unpredictable things to happen and the range of likely stock price increases. Moreover, the more time the option holder has, the lower the present value of the exercise price (thus increasing the option value). Like volatility, time to expiration increases the value of both put and call options.

- Interest rates. If interest rates are higher, the exercise price has a lower present value. This also increases the value of the option.

- Dividends. A higher dividend rate policy of the company means that out of the total expected return on the stock, some is being delivered in the form of dividends. This means that the capital gain the stock can be expected to get will be lower, and the potential increase in stock price is lower. Hence, larger dividend payouts lower the call value.

The following table summarizes the relationships between these factors and the value of options:

If this variable increases	The value of a call option
Stock price	Increases
Exercise price	Decreases
Volatility	Increases
Time to expiration	Increases
Interest rate	Increases
Dividend payouts	Increases

In the end, the price of an option, like any security, is determined by the market. However, as with the various valuation techniques for companies disccused previously, there are standard methods of pricing options, most prominently the Black-Scholes model. This model has essentially become the industry standard, and is a fairly good predictor of how the market prices options.

Those interviewing for jobs as derivative traders should consult a finance textbook and understand the model in further detail, as interviewers for these position are bound to ask more detailed questions based on the Black-Scholes model and its application.

Forwards, futures, and swaps

Other popular derivatives instruments include forwards, futures, and swaps.

Forwards

A **forward** contract is an agreement that calls for future delivery of an asset at an agreed-upon price. Let's say a farmer grows a single crop, wheat. The revenue from the entire planting season depends critically on the highly volatile price of wheat. The farmer can't easily diversify his position because virtually his entire wealth is tied up in the crop. The miller who must purchase wheat for processing faces a portfolio problem that is a mirror image of the farmer's. He is subject to profit uncertainty because of the unpredictable future of the wheat price when the day comes for him to buy his wheat.

Both parties can reduce their risk if they enter into a forward contract requiring the farmer to deliver the wheat at a previously agreed upon price, regardless of what the market price is at harvest time. No money needs to change hands at the time the agreement is made. A forward contract is simply a deferred delivery sale of some asset with an agreed-upon sales price. The contract is designed to protect each party from future price fluctuations.

These forwards are generally used by large companies that deal with immense quantities of commodities, like Cargill or Archer Daniels Midland.

Futures

The **futures** contract is a type of forward that calls for the delivery of an asset or its cash value at a specified delivery or maturity date for an agreed upon price. This price is called the futures price, and is to be paid when the contract matures. The trader who commits to purchasing the commodity on the delivery date is said to be in the "**long position**." The trader who takes the "**short position**" commits to delivering the commodity when the contract matures.

Futures differ from other forwards in the fact that they are liquid, standardized, traded on an exchange, and their prices are settled at the end of each trading day (that is, the futures traders collect/pay their day's gains and losses at the end of each day). Futures are actively traded and liquid securities. For example, for agricultural commodities, the exchange sets allowable grades of a commodity (for example, No. 2 hard winter wheat or No. 1 soft red wheat). The place or means of delivery of the commodity is specified as issued by approved warehouses. The dates of delivery are also standardized. The prices of the major agricultural futures appear in *The Wall Street Journal*. Futures are also available on other commodities, like gold and oil.

Swaps

Another derivative, a **swap**, is a simple exchange of future cash flows. Some popular forms of swaps include foreign exchange swaps and interest rate swaps. Let's first examine foreign exchange swaps.

Say Sun Microsystems outsources its software development to India on a regular basis. In such a situation, it would make payments to the firms in India in rupees, thus find itself exposed to foreign exchange rate fluctuation risks. To hedge these exchange risks, Sun would want to enter into a foreign exchange swap — a predetermined exchange of currency — with another party. For example, Sun might want to swap $1.0 million for Rs 40 million for each of the next five years. For instance, it could enter into a swap with the Birla Group in India, which has many expenses in U.S. dollars and is thus also subject to the same exchange rate fluctuation risk. By agreeing to a foreign exchange swap, both companies protect their business from exchange rate risks.

Interest rate swaps work similarly. Consider a firm (Company A) that has issued bonds (which, remember, means essentially that it has taken loans) with a total par value of $10 million at a fixed interest rate of 8%. By issuing the bonds, the firm is obligated to pay a fixed interest rate of $800,000 at the end of each year. In a situation like this, it can enter into an interest rate swap with another party (Company B), where Company A pays Company B the LIBOR rate (a floating, or variable, short-term interest rate measure) and Company B agrees to pay Company A the fixed rate. In such a case, Company A would receive $800,000 each year that it could use to make its loan payment. For its part, Company A would be obligated to pay $10 million x LIBOR each year to Company B. Hence Company A has swapped its fixed interest rate debt to a floating rate debt. (The company swaps rates with Company B, called the "counterparty." The counterparty gains because presumably it wants to swap its floating rate debt for fixed rate debt, thus "locking in" a fixed rate.) The chart below illustrates this swap.

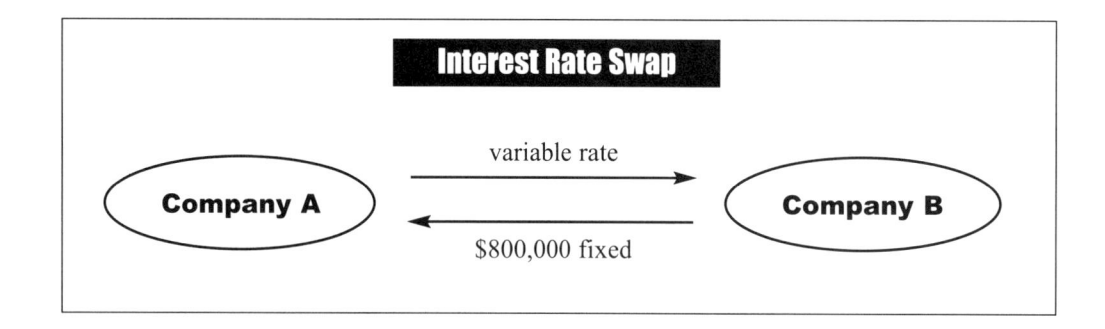

Interest Rate Swap

Company A → variable rate → Company B
Company A ← $800,000 fixed ← Company B

Questions

1. When would you write a call option on Disney stock?

When you expect the price of Disney stock to fall (or stay the same). Because a call option on a stock is a bet that the value of the stock will increase, you would be willing to "write" (sell) a call option on Disney stock to an investor if you believed Disney stock would not rise. (In this case, the profit you would make would be equal to the option premium you received when you sold the option.)

2. Explain how a swap works.

A swap is an exchange of future cash flows. The most popular forms include foreign exchange swaps and interest rate swaps. They are used to hedge volatile rates, such as currency exchange rates or interest rates.

3. Say I hold a put option on Amazon.com stock with an exercise price of $250, the expiration date is today, and Amazon is trading at $220. About how much is my put worth, and why?

Your put is worth about $30, because today, you can sell a share of stock for $250, and buy it for $220. (If the expiration date were in the future, the option would be more valuable, because the stock could conceivably drop more.)

4. When would a trader seeking profit from a long-term possession of a future be in the "long position"?

The trader in the long position is committed to buying a commodity on a delivery date. She would hold this position if she believes the commodity price will increase.

Options & Derivatives

5. All else being equal, which would be less valuable: a December put option on AOL stock or a December put option on Bell Atlantic stock?

The put option on Bell Atlantic should be less valuable. AOL is a more volatile stock, and the more volatile the underlying asset, the more valuable the option.

6. All else being equal, which would be more valuable: a December call option for eBay or a January call option for eBay?

The January option: The later an option's expiration date, the more valuable the option.

7. Why do interest rates matter when figuring the price of options?

Because of the ever-important concept of net present value, higher interest rates lower the value of options.

8. If the strike price on a put option is below the current price, is the option holder at the money, in the money or out of the money?

Because a put option gives the holder the right to sell a security at a certain price, the fact that the strike (or exercise) price is below the current price would mean that the option holder would lose money. Translate that knowledge into option lingo, and you know that the option holder is "out of the money."

9. If the current price of a stock is above the strike price of a call option, is the option holder at the money, in the money, or out of the money?

Because a call option gives the holder the right to buy a security, the holder in this scenario is "in the money" (making money).

10. When would you buy a put option on Time Warner stock?

Because buying a put option gives you the option to sell the stock at a certain price, you would do this if you expect the price of Time Warner stock to fall.

Mergers & Acquisitions

We have seemingly entered an age in which virtually every week, we are greeted with news of blockbuster, bigger-than-ever-before mergers like those between Mobil and Exxon and Deutsche Bank and Bankers Trust. In fact, the seven largest mergers ever — and eight of the largest 10 — were announced in 1998. Why are companies in industries ranging from telecommunications to financial services to retail looking to merge? Because of the much referred to "synergies" that theoretically result from a merger. Because of synergies, the combination of the two companies that merge are thought to be greater than the sum of the two independently. Examples of these synergies include: reductions in redundant workforce, and utilizing the technology and market share of the other party to the deal. Let's take a look at the major reasons for M&A activity.

Why merge?

One important reason that a company might merge with another company is to gain footholds in new markets. In some cases, companies gain entry to new product markets, or add products complimentary to their business lines. For example, in the Salomon/Smith Barney merger, Salomon Brothers gained an immense brokerage army to hawk the bonds and stocks it underwrites. Smith Barney gained a leading investment bank that can originate financial products. Merging to add new product lines is a strong reason for the big push in media/telecom mergers — as the telecommunications industry deregulates, telecom companies are looking for ways to put together Internet access and long distance service, local lines and cable access.

In other cases, companies merge to enter new geographic markets. Chrysler sells its cars almost exclusively in North America; Daimler-Benz is strong in Europe. Thus the two agree to combine and form DaimlerChrysler.

Sometimes mergers are driven by the coveted brand recognition of the acquisition. For example, by acquiring US Robotics, 3Com added US Robotics' strong brand recognition in the modem industry. (That merger also added an important hardware strength to 3Com's drive to challenge Cisco as the computer networking leader.)

In other cases, companies merge to consolidate operations, thus lowering costs and boosting profits (think "economies of scale"). Why pay for two legal departments, two PR departments, or two headquarters when you only need one? Moreover, if you can buy 10,000 sheets of metal for less than you can buy 5,000, maybe you should merge with someone who would gain the same advantage.

And sometimes, companies merge just to get bigger in a consolidating industry. In some industries, most notably banking and brokerage, executives believe that size is required in order to compete as the industry consolidates around a handful of major players.

Why not merge?

While mergers are fun and exciting to talk about, the post-merger logistics aren't always as sexy. Did you know that more than one out of every five mergers does not achieve the synergies initially targeted? This isn't just because of poor implementation after the merger. Many mergers are simply ill-advised or involve a clash of corporate cultures.

So why do they go through? One reason is that many mergers are also the result of management egos and the excitement generated in a merger mania market. For example, the recent Mobil/Exxon deal was constructed largely in private through the efforts of the CEOs of the two companies, Lucio Noto of Mobil and Lee Raymond of Exxon. (This is not to say that this merger will not work, but to simply note that it, like many mergers, was driven by the personalities and choices of individuals.)

Another powerful force pushing mergers are the huge I-banking fees that the deals generate. Investment bankers are going to argue to their clients that the mergers are in their best interest because they are in fact in *their* (the bankers') best interest. Goldman Sachs and Credit Suisse First Boston both pocketed about $30 million from their advisory roles in the AT&T/TCI merger. Think they didn't have some incentive to be enthusiastic when talking about telecom/cable TV synergy?

Stock swaps vs. cash offers

Bankers and finance officials at companies have a couple of main options when they consider how to structure a merger: a stock swap or a cash deal. The most common type of deal these days is a stock swap — when the stock of one company is exchanged for the stock of another. Cash offers occur when one company pays cash for the stock of another.

The reason for the current reliance on stock swaps is the strong stock market, which makes it easier for a company with a high market capitalization to acquire companies. It can use its valuable stock, rather than cash, to merge with or acquire companies. According to *Fortune* magazine, 67% of the merger activity in 1998 was accomplished through stock, versus 33% through cash. In 1988, the ratio was only 7% stock to 93% cash. Of course, the volatility of the stock market can make stock swaps tricky. We should understand why many announced mergers become "pending" once the stock market crashes — the initial assumptions for valuing the companies are not true anymore when the market falls. Interestingly, when the market is good or bullish, the merger mania heightens! Even though valuations are inflated, the environment is optimistic and it looks like both companies made off well — the acquired company is given a very high market value, while the acquirer appears to have gained valuable assets.

In a cash deal, shareholders must pay taxes when they receive the cash. The tax rate for their earnings is at the ordinary income marginal tax rate (your tax rate increases as the income bracket you are in goes higher), which is 39.6% for wealthy individuals. By contrast, in a stock swap, no taxes are paid at the time of the swap. But when the swapped stock is sold in the market, the shareholder must pay capital gains tax at a marginal tax rate of 20%. The U.S. government sets tax laws this way as a part of its fiscal strategy to regulate the amount of cash in the economy and to control factors like inflation.

Type of Merger	1988	1998
Stock	7%	67%
Cash	93%	33%

Source: Fortune *magazine*

Tender offers

Tender offers are associated with hostile takeovers. In a tender offer, the hostile acquirer renders a tender to the public in an attempt to gather a controlling interest in (majority ownership of) a company. For example, let's say Mr. T-Bone Pickins wants to take over Acme Internet Corp., and that Acme stock is trading at $20 per share. Say Pickins issues an advertisement to the public — usually through the newspaper, or sometimes through direct mail campaigns — that announces that he will buy Acme stock for $40 a share (double the going market price). If he can garner 51% of the stock outstanding through this method, he will also have gained controlling ownership of the stock.

When a tender offer is issued, the share price generally shoots right up to offering price — in our example, to $40 per share. (If it didn't, I, as T-Bone Pickins, would simply buy from the market, rather than following though with the tender offer, wouldn't I? Or better still, if the stock price didn't rise, I, as John Doe investor, would simply buy from the market and sell to T-Bone.)

However, Pickins doesn't have to buy all the stock offered to him through a tender offer. If he receives offers for more than 75% of the stock and doesn't want to buy more than 51%, he can buy 2/3 of the stock that each shareholder offers him. For example, if you were an Acme shareholder interested in T-Bone's offer, and were willing to sell him your 1,000 shares, he would only buy 2/3 of your stock (666 shares) for $40 and the other 1/3 for $20. (The consequence of this, of course, is that you would only sell him 2/3 of your shares.) Also, because he has made a tender offer, if Pickins does not receive offers to buy 51% at his price, he does not have to purchase the shares offered to him.

Why would anyone offer $40 a share to buy a company that the market valued at only $20 a share? Basically, if they believe they can do substantially better with the company than current management — whether because of expected synergies with companies they already own, a belief that the company is inefficient and mismanaged, a belief the company is worth more in parts than as a whole, or any other reason they believe the company's inherent assets to be substantially more valuable than its current market value. (All the reasons together result in the "control premium," or the premium over the current value.)

Of course, the target company can defend itself. Say Acme's management hires Wasserstein Purella to make a counter bid to prevent a hostile takeover and offers another tender at a even higher price. Sometimes this leads to an auction situation (the famous RJR Nabisco case is an example of an escalating auction, although no tenders were involved there).

Mergers vs. acquisitions

The terms "merger" and "acquisition" are often used loosely and interchangeably. For example, a bit of tension arose in the recent Bankers Trust/Deutsche Bank deal when Deutsche Bank officials became irked at Bankers Trust execs' continual referral to the deal as a merger when it was in fact an acquisition.

When two companies of relatively equal size decide to combine forces, it is usually referred to as a "merger of equals." Examples of this type of deal are the recent BP/Amoco merger, or the Morgan Stanley/Dean Witter, Travelers Group/Citibank, and Daimler-Benz/Chrysler mergers. On the other hand, if one company buys out another, the deal is considered a purchase or acquisition. Examples of this include AOL's acquisition of Netscape or Nortel's acquisition of Bay Networks.

Despite this sometimes loose definition of how we normally categorize mergers and acquisitions, there are real legal and accounting differences between the two — which, it ends up, basically depend on the method used for the transaction (stock swap, etc. as discussed above).

Whether a deal is a "merger" or an "acquisition" determines the taxes paid because of the combination. Whenever there is a combination of two firms, the financial statements of the two firms need to be combined. These can be combined using either "pooling" or "purchase" accounting. Whether a combination can be accounted using "pooling" methods depends on a complex list of rules. (In the U.S., these rules are FASB rules, referred to as fas-B rules. Although the U.S. is trying to impose FASB regulations worldwide, it is facing stiff opposition.) The simplest, most general way to explain these rules is that if the deal is a stock-for-stock deal, it can be accounted using pooling accounting. If the deal involves a considerable amount of cash (traded for the stock of a company), it must to be accounted using purchase accounting.

We love pooling accounting

Investment bankers and the finance departments of merging companies always prefer to use **pooling accounting** rather than **purchase accounting**. Why? Because there is no "**Goodwill**" when one accounts for a merger using pooling techniques. "Goodwill" is an account that represents some of the intangible assets a company may have. (Other intangible assets include patents and copyrights.) For example, the public image of a company, and the financial value that image adds, is included in Goodwill. If a company is considered sexy and desirable (say a company like Mercedes-Benz or Coca-Cola), an acquirer of the company may be willing to pay for this image (which presumably translates into sales).

To define the Goodwill created during a purchase accounting merger more strictly, we can say that it is the price paid over the Net Market Value of the assets of the company being acquired.

Mergers & Acquisitions

> **Goodwill** = Price paid - Net Market Value of Assets
>
> **Net Market Value of Assets** = Market Value of Assets + Market Value of Debt

The reason those involved in an M&A deal would rather not account for Goodwill is that the Goodwill account, like all others, must be amortized and be recorded as an amortization expense. This cuts into the projected future earnings of the firm and thereby the market valuation (as determined by P/E multiples). In order to avoid creating a Goodwill account, investment bankers and M&A accountants are always on the lookout for loopholes that will allow them to use pooling accounting instead of purchase accounting.

Let's take a look at an example to illustrate the difference between pooling and purchase accounting. Here, Company P is acquiring Company S. In our example, Company P swaps 250 of its shares for all 500 Shares of S. Just before the swap, Company P's Shares have a Market Value of $1.50 per share. Here's an overview:

	Company P	Company S Book Value	Company S Market Value
Assets	700	350	450
Liabilities	300	150	100
Common Stock	150	75	
Retained Earnings	250	125	

Purchase accounting

If this deal would be accounted using purchase accounting, the acquisition price is the amount of stock given multiplied by its price, or 250 x $1.50 = $375. But the Net Market Value of Company S's assets is only $350. The difference ($25) is considered Goodwill.

> Money paid = $375
> - Net Market Value of Assets = $350
> Goodwill generated = $25

On the Balance Sheet of the combined company, the Market Value of Company S's assets and liabilities will be added to the Book Value of P's assets and liabilities. (S's assets and liabilities are said to be "stepped up to market" value. The final Balance Sheet of the merged company looks like:

Assets	$1,150	(700 + 450)
		Assets "stepped up to market"
Goodwill	+ $25	
	$1,175	
Liabilities	$450	(300 + 100)
Common Stock	$525	(150 + 375)
Retained Earnings	$250	
	$1,175	

The $25 in Goodwill will be amortized over a period of time and will show up in the Income Statement as Depreciation and Amortization and thereby reduce the combined company's earnings.

Pooling accounting

If this deal were done through pooling accounting, the purchase price would be accounted as the Book Value of S's Net Assets, or $350 - $150 = $200. Also, there would be no Goodwill generated, and the Assets and Liabilities would be recorded at Book Value.

The final Balance Sheet of the combined company would look like:

Assets	$1,050	($700 + $350)
Goodwill	0	
	$1,050	
Liabilities	$450	(300 + 150)
Common Stock	$225	(150 + 75)
Retained Earnings	$375	(250 + 125)
	$1,050	

Will that be cash or stock?

The choice of whether to make a cash deal or stock swap depends largely on the tax factors discussed above. However, it can also depend on other factors. For example, if the stockholders of the company being acquired value the stock of their acquirer and believe that the merged company will be a long-term industry leader (and is thus a company whose stock they would like to receive), they will push for a stock swap. On the other hand, the volatility of the stock market must also be considered; if the market is behaving like a roller coaster, a company's board of directors and shareholders may feel they can not stomach a stock swap, and opt for a cash deal. Another factor that may come into play is how soon an acquired company will receive cash in a cash deal, and how badly it needs the cash. If we remember our discussion of net present value, we know that cash today is worth more than cash tomorrow.

Accretive vs. dilutive mergers

A merger can be either **accretive** or **dilutive**. A merger is accretive when the acquiring company's earnings per share will increase after the merger. A merger is dilutive when the acquiring company's earnings will fall after a merger.

Let's take a look at an example. Say a shoe company, Big Gun wants to acquire a fast growing competitor, Ubershoe. Also suppose that Big Gun's earnings are $10 million, that it has 1 million outstanding shares (and thus has earnings of $10 per share), and that Ubershoe's earnings are $2 million.

Whether the acquisition will be accretive or dilutive depends on the amount Big Gun will pay for Ubershoe. Say that Big Gun agrees to a stock swap in which it issues 500,000 shares which it will trade for all of Ubershoe's shares. The combined company will have 1.5 million shares and $12 million in earnings. The new earnings per share are $8 per share. This deal is dilutive to Big Gun's earnings.

But say that the terms of the acquisition are different, and Big Gun agrees to issue 100,000 new shares of stock instead of 500,000. The combined company will have $12 million in earnings and 1.1 million shares, or earnings of $10.91 per share. This deal is accretive to Big Gun's earnings.

Figuring out whether a merger is accretive or dilutive can be done by actually adding up the companies' earnings and shares (as we have done in this case), but an easier way is to use the companies' price to earnings ratios (P/Es). The rule is this: When a company with a higher price to earnings ratio (we'll call the company "Company 1," and label it's P/E ratio "P/E_1") acquires a firm, "Company 2" of a lower P/E ratio (which we will label P/E_2), it is an accretive merger.

If Company 1 acquires Company 2

Earnings Relationship	Merger Type
$P/E_1 > P/E_2$	Accretive
$P/E_1 < P/E_2$	Dilutive

Vault.com Guide to Finance Interviews
Mergers & Acquisitions

Questions

1. Describe a recent M&A transaction that you've read about.

If you are preparing for an I-banking interview, this is a must prepare question. Read the papers and have at least one transaction thoroughly prepared. You should be able to cover various aspects of the transactions. You should know what the structure of the transaction was. Who was buying whom, or was it a merger of equals? Was it an all-stock transaction or was there cash involved?

For example, you could talk about America Online's acquisition of Netscape. In that transaction, a stock swap valued at $4.2 billion, AOL acquired Netscape. You should talk about how the acquisition was structured from a financial point of view, and the effect the acquisition is likely to have on AOL's earnings (both short-term and long-term).

2. What were the reasons behind that transaction? Does that transaction make sense?

Perhaps more important than understanding the nuts and bolts mechanics of transactions is understanding the factors that drive M&A activity. The America Online/Netscape deal is especially interesting in this regard because it involves heavy strategic planning in a fast-moving industry (as opposed to, say, the merger between Mobil and Exxon, through which the two giants simply hope to consolidate, save, and boost profits).

America Online is a content-driven company with more than 16 million subscribers. Netscape has popular software, in the form of a popular browser and tools for businesses to pursue e-commerce. However, Netscape has seen its browser market share fall as Microsoft, with its immense distribution strength (and questionable pairing of browser with operating system) has elbowed its way into the category. And despite America Online's undisputed lead in market share as an Internet service provider, it had not moved aggressively into what many consider to be the golden road of the Internet e-commerce.

This deal partners AOL and Netscape with Sun Microsystems, which is a hardware company that boasts strong hardware products and sales and support staff. The partners envision a world in which companies use the e-commerce tools developed by Netscape, hawk their wares on America Online (lured by the audience AOL can deliver), and are supported in their hardware and service needs by Sun. Synergy for the 21st century.

Again, your interviewer will expect you to discuss both the financial structure of a deal, its impact on earnings, as well as its strategic drivers.

3. Do you know whether most mergers are stock swaps or cash transactions and why?

These days, most mergers are stock swaps, largely because the stock prices of companies are so high. In addition, stock swaps generally permit the acquirer to use pooling accounting to account for the merger.

4. When can you use pooling accounting?

Most generally, when a transaction is legally a merger, or a stock swap.

5. What is a dilutive merger?

A merger in which the acquiring company's earnings per share decreases as a result of the merger. Also remember the P/E rule: A dilutive merger happens when a company with a lower P/E ratio acquires a company with a higher P/E ratio.

6. What is an accretive merger?

The type of merger in which the acquiring's earnings per share increase. With regard to P/E ratio, this happens when a company with a higher P/E ratio acquires a company with a lower P/E ratio. The acquiring company's earnings per share should rise following the merger.

7. Company A is considering acquiring Company B. Company A's P/E ratio is 55 times earnings, whereas Company B's P/E ratio is 30 times earnings. After Company A acquires Company B, will Company A's earnings per share rise, fall, or stay the same?

Company A's earnings per share will rise, because of the following rule: When a higher P/E company buys a lower P/E company, the acquirer's earnings-per-share will rise. The deal is said to be "accretive," as opposed to "dilutive," to the acquirer's earnings.

Vault.com Guide to Finance Interviews
Mergers & Acquisitions

8. Can you name two companies that you think should merge?

Identifying "synergies" between two companies is only part of correctly answering this question. You also need to ensure that the merger will not raise antitrust issues with FTC. For example, you could say that Apple and Microsoft should merge, but the combined company will have an unfair monopoly on the operating system market and the FTC will not approve the merger. Moreover, the top people running the two companies don't like each other and would not want to merge!

9. What is a hostile tender offer?

If company A wants to acquire company B, but company B refuses, company A can "issue a tender offering." In this offer, company A will take advertisements in major newspapers like *The Wall Street Journal* to buy stock in company B at a price much above the market price. If company A is able to get more than 50% of the stock that way, it can officially run and make all major decisions for company B — including firing the top management. This is something of a simplistic view; there are scores of rules and regulations from the SEC governing such activity.

10. What is a leveraged buyout? How is it different than a merger?

A leveraged buyout occurs when a group, by refinancing a company with debt, is able to increase the valuation of the company. LBOs are typically accomplished by either financial groups such as KKR or company management, whereas M&A deals are led by companies in the industry.

11. If Company A buys Company B, what will the Balance Sheet of the combined company look like?

In this accounting, simply add each line item on the Balance Sheet.

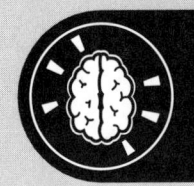

Brainteasers & Guesstimates

Perhaps even more so than tough finance questions, brainteasers and guesstimates can unnerve the most icy-veined, well-prepared finance candidate. Even if you know the relationships between inflation, bond prices and interest rates like the back of a dollar bill, all your studying may not help you when your interviewer asks you how many ping pong balls fit in a 747.

That is partly their purpose. Investment bankers and other finance professionals need to be able to work well under pressure, so many interviewers believe that throwing a brainteaser or guesstimate at a candidate is a good way to test an applicant's battle-worthiness. But these questions serve another purpose, too — interviewers want you to showcase your ability to analyze a situation, and to form conclusions about this situation. It is not usually important that you come up with a "correct" answer, just that you display strong analytical ability

Acing guesstimates

We'll start by discussing guesstimates, for which candidates are asked to come up with a figure, usually the size of a market or the number of objects in an area. Although guesstimates are more commonly given in interviews for consulting positions, they do pop up in finance interviews as well. Also, they are a good way to begin preparing for stress questions in finance interviews, as they force candidates to think aloud — precisely what interviewers want to see. This is the most important thing to remember about brainteasers, guesstimates, or even simple math questions that are designed to be stressful: Let your interviewer see how your mind works.

The best approach for a guesstimate question is to think of a funnel. You begin by thinking broadly, then slowly narrowing down the situation towards the answer. Let's look at this approach in context. Let's go back to the question of how many ping pong balls fit in a 747. The first thing you need to determine is the volume of the ping pong ball.

For any guesstimate or brainteaser question, you will need to understand whether your interviewer will be providing any direction or whether you will have to make assumptions. Therefore, begin the analysis of a guesstimate or brainteaser question with a question to your interviewer, such as, "What is the volume of a single ping pong ball?" If the interviewer does not know or refuses to provide any answer, then you will know that you must assume the answer. If they do provide the information, then your approach will be a series of questions. For this example let's assume your interviewer wants you to make the assumptions. Your verbal dialogue might go something like this:

"Let's assume that the volume of a ping pong ball is three cubic inches. Now let's assume that all the seats in the plane are removed. I know that an average refrigerator is about 23 cubic feet, and you could probably fit two average people in the space occupied by that refrigerator, so let's say that the volume of an average person is 12 cubic feet, or 144 cubic inches.

Okay, so a 747 has about 400 seats in it, excluding the galleys, lavatories, and aisles on the lower deck and about 25 seats on the upper deck. Let's assume there are three galleys, 14 lavatories, and three aisles (two on the lower deck and one on the upper deck) and that the space occupied by the galleys is a six-person equivalent, by the lavatories is a two-person equivalent, and the aisles are a 50-person equivalent on the lower deck and a 20-person equivalent on the upper deck. That's an additional 18, 28, and 120 person-volumes for the remaining space. We won't include the cockpit since someone has to fly the plane. So there are about 600 person-equivalents available.

In addition to the human volume, we have to take into account all the cargo and extra space — the belly holds, the overhead luggage compartments, and the space over the passengers' head. Let's assume the plane holds four times the amount of extra space as it does people, so that would mean extra space is 2,400 person-equivalents in volume. (Obviously, this assumption is the most important factor in this guesstimate. Remember that it's not important that this assumption be correct, just that you know the assumption should be made.)

Therefore, in total we have 3,000 (or 600 + 2,400) person-equivalents in volume available. Three thousand x 144 cubic inches means we have 432,000 cubic inches of space available. At three cubic inches per ball, a 747 could hold 144,000 balls. However, spheres do not fit perfectly together. Eliminate a certain percentage — spheres lose about 30 percent when packed — and cut your answer to 100,800.

You might be wondering how you would calculate all these numbers in your head! No one expects you to be a human calculator, so you should be writing down these numbers as you develop them. Then you can do the math on paper, in front of the interviewer, which will further demonstrate your analytical abilities.

You choose the numbers, so pick nice round numbers that are easy for you to manipulate. Even if you just read a study that states that there are 270 million people in the United States, no interviewer will flinch if you estimate the number of Americans as 300 million.

Note: The extra step

Don't forget to add the "extra step" that often pop into guesstimates. In our previous example, this step involved reducing our estimate of ping pong balls because spheres do not pack perfectly together. If you're trying to figure out how many blocks there are in New York City, remember to eliminate blocks covered by Central Park (and other parks). If you're determining the number of black cars in the United States, once you've estimated the number of cars in America, make sure you estimate what percentage of them are black.

Brainteasers

Now we'll turn our attention to brainteasers, which are often used in finance interviews. Some of these, like the legendary "Why is the manhole round?" question which reportedly originated at Microsoft, have no definite answer. Others do have answers, but even with these, interviewers are more interested in assessing creativity, composure, and your ability to deconstruct a problem and ask directed and relevant questions.

Remember, brainteasers are very unstructured, so it is tough to suggest a step-by-step methodology as we can with guesstimates. There are a couple of set rules, though. First, take notes as your interviewer gives you a brainteaser, especially if it's heavy on the math. Second, think aloud so your interviewer can hear your thought process. This may seem unnatural at first; the examples at the end of this chapter will show you how to logically attack these questions, and how you should vocalize your analysis.

Quick: What's 2 + 2

In addition to the riddle-type brainteasers, finance interviewers will often throw out simple mathematical questions designed to see how quick thinking you are. The math questions are most often given to analyst applicants. The best way to prepare for these (other than to find out which of these questions are most common, which we've happily done for you), is simply to know that you might get one of them. That way, if you do, you won't be quite as surprised or unprepared.

… Brainteasers & Guesstimates

Questions

1. How many gallons of white housepaint are sold in the U.S. every year?

THE "START BIG" APPROACH: If you're not sure where to begin, start with the basic assumption that there are 270 million people in the U.S. (or 25 million businesses, depending on the question). If there are 270 million people in the United States, perhaps half of them live in houses (or 135 million people). The average family size is about three people, so there would be 45 million houses in the United States. Let's add another 10 percent to that for second houses and houses used for other purposes besides residential. So there are about 50 million houses.

If houses are painted every 10 years, on average (notice how we deftly make that number easy to work with), then there are 5 million houses painted every year. Assuming that one gallon of paint covers 100 square feet of wall, and that the average house has 2,000 square feet of wall to cover, then each house needs 20 gallons of paint. So 100 million gallons of paint are sold per year (5 million houses x 20 gallons). (Note: If you want to be fancy, you can ask your interviewer whether you should include inner walls as well!) If 80 percent of all houses are white, then 80 million gallons of white housepaint are sold each year. (Don't forget that last step!)

THE "START SMALL" APPROACH: You could also start small, and take a town of 27,000 (about one ten thousandth of the population). If you use the same assumption that half the town lives in houses in groups of three, then there are 4,500 houses, plus another 10 percent, then there are really 5,000 houses to worry about. Painted every 10 years, 500 houses are being painted in any given year. If each house has 2,000 square feet of wall, and each gallon of paint covers 100 square feet, then each house needs 20 gallons — and so 10,000 gallons of housepaint are sold each year in your typical town. Perhaps 8,000 of those are white. Multiply by 10,000 — you have 80 million gallons.

Your interviewer may then ask you how you would actually get that number, on the job, if necessary. Use your creativity — contacting major paint producers would be smart, putting in a call to HUD's statistics arm could help, or even conducting a small sample of the second calculation in a few representative towns is possible.

2. What is the size of the market for disposable diapers in China?

Here's a good example of a market sizing. How many people live in China? A billion. Because the population of China is young, a full 600 million of those inhabitants might be of child-bearing age. Half are women, so there are about 300 million Chinese women of childbearing age. Now, the average family size in China is restricted, so it might be 1.5 children, on average, per family. Let's say two-thirds of Chinese women have children. That means that there are about 200 million children in China. How many of those kids are under the age of two? About a tenth, or 20 million. So there are at least 20 million possible consumers of disposable diapers.

To summarize:

      1 billion people
x   60% childbearing age
=   600,000,000 people
x $^1/_2$ are women

=   300,000,00 women of childbearing age
x $^2/_3$ have children

=   200,000,000 women with children
x   1.5 children each

=   300,000,000 children
x $^1/_{10}$ under age 2

=   30 million

3. How many square feet of pizza are eaten in the United States each month?

Take your figure of 300 million people in America. How many people eat pizza? Let's say 200 million. Now let's say the average pizza-eating person eats pizza twice a month, and eats two slices at a time. That's four slices a month. If the average slice of pizza is perhaps six inches at the base and 10 inches long, then the slice is 30 square inches of pizza. So four pizza slices would be 120 square inches. Therefore, there are a billion square feet of pizza eaten every month.

To summarize:

- 300 million people in America
- 200 million eat pizza
- Average slice of pizza is six inches at the base and 10 inches long = 30 square inches (height x half the base)
- Average American eats four slices of pizza a month
- Four pieces x 30 square inches = 120 square inches (one square foot is 144 inches), so let's assume one square foot a person
- 200 million square feet a month

4. How many pay phones are there on the island of Manhattan?

There are two ways to handle this problem. First of all, you could estimate how many blocks there are in Manhattan, and assume that 75 percent of all blocks have a pay phone. (Remember, the interviewer didn't say they had to work.) If there are about 15 avenues across Manhattan, and if the island is 300 streets long, then there are about 4500 intersections. If every intersection indicates a block, then there are 4500 blocks in the city. That means 3000 pay phones. Now add the extra step and subtract the size of Central Park. Say that Central Park is 50 streets by six avenues — that means you lose 300 blocks, or 200 pay phones. You have the figure of 2800 pay phones. Now estimate how many pay phones exist in bars, restaurants, schools, etc. There may be a total of 3500 pay phones in Manhattan. (This question is also sometimes used with estimating the number of manhole covers in Manhattan.)

5. How would you estimate the weight of the Chrysler building?

This is a process guesstimate — the interviewer wants to know if you know what questions to ask. First, you would find out the dimensions of the building (height, weight, depth). This will allow you to determine the volume of the building. Does it taper at the top? (Yes.) Then, you need to estimate the composition of the Chrysler building. Is it mostly steel? Concrete? How much would those components weigh per square inch? Remember the extra step — find out whether you're considering the building totally empty or with office furniture, people, etc.

6. Why are manhole covers round?

The classic brainteaser, brought straight to you via Microsoft (the originator). Even though this question has been around for yours, interviewees still encounter it. Here's how to "solve" this brainteaser. Remember to speak and reason out loud while solving this brainteaser!

Why are manhole covers round? Could there be a structural reason? Why aren't manhole covers square? It would make it harder to fit with a cover. You'd have to rotate it exactly the right way. So many manhole covers are round because they don't need to be rotated. There are no corners to deal with. Also, a round manhole cover won't fall into a hole if it is rotated the wrong way, so it's safer.

Looking at this, it seems corners are a problem. You can't cut yourself on a round manhole cover. And because it's round, it can be more easily transported. One person can roll it.

7. If you look at a clock and the time is 3:15, what is the angle between the hour and the minute hands?

The answer to this is not zero! The hour hand, remember, moves as well. The hour hand moves a quarter of the way between three and four, so it moves a quarter of a twelfth ($1/48$) of 360 degrees. So the answer is seven and a half degrees, to be exact.

8. You have a five-gallon jug and a three-gallon jug. You must obtain exactly four gallons of water. How will you do it?

You should find this brainteaser fairly simple. If you were to think out loud, you might begin by examining the ways in which combinations of five and three can come up to be four. For example: (5 - 3) + (5 - 3) = 4. This path does not actually lead to the right answer, but it is a fruitful way to begin thinking about the question. Here's the solution: fill the three-gallon jug with water and pour it into the five-gallon jug. Repeat. Because you can only put two more gallons into the five-gallon jug, one gallon will be left over in the three-gallon jug. Empty out the five-gallon jug and pour in the one gallon. Now just fill the three-gallon jug again and pour it into the five-gallon jug. Ta-da. (Mathematically, this can be represented 3 + 3 - 5 + 3 = 4)

9. You have 12 balls. All of them are identical except one, which is either heavier or lighter than the rest. The odd ball is either hollow while the rest are solid, or solid while the rest are hollow. You have a scale, and are permitted three weighings. Can you identify the odd ball, and determine whether it is hollow or solid?

This is a pretty complex question, and there are actually multiple solutions. First, we'll examine what thought processes an interviewer is looking for, and then we'll discuss one solution.

Start with the simplest of observations. The number of balls you weigh against each other must be equal. Yeah, it's obvious, but why? Because if you weigh, say three balls against five, you are not receiving any information. In a problem like this, you are trying to receive as much information as possible with each weighing.

For example, one of the first mistakes people make when examining this problem is that they believe the first weighing should involve all of the balls (six against six). This weighing involves all of the balls, but what type of information does this give you? It actually gives you no new information. You already know that one of the sides will be heavier than the other, and by weighing six against six, you will simply confirm this knowledge. Still, you want to gain information about as many balls as possible (so weighing one against one is obviously not a good idea). Thus the best first weighing is four against four.

Secondly, if you think through this problem long enough, you will realize how precious the information gained from a weighing is: You need to transfer virtually every piece of information you have gained from one weighing to the next. Say you weigh four against four, and the scale balances. Lucky you! Now you know that the odd ball is one of the unweighed four. But don't give into the impulse to simply work with those balls. In this weighing, you've also learned that the eight balls on the scale are normal. Try to use this information.

Finally, remember to use your creativity. Most people who work through this problem consider only weighing a number of balls against each other, and then taking another set and weighing them, etc. This won't do. There are a number of other types of moves you can make — you can rotate the balls from one scale to another, you can switch the balls, etc.

Let's look at one solution:

For simplicity's sake, we will refer to one side of the scale as Side A, and the other as Side B.

Step 1: Weigh four balls against four others.

Case A: If, on the first weighing, the balls balance

If the balls in our first weighing balance we know the odd ball is one of those not weighed, but we don't know whether it is heavy or light. How can we gain this information easily? We can weigh them against the balls we know to be normal. So:

Step 2: Put three of the unweighed balls on the Side A; put three balls that are known to be normal on Side B.

> I. If on this second weighing, the scale balances again, we know that the final unweighed ball is the odd one.

Step 3a: Weigh the final unweighed ball (the odd one) against one of the normal balls. With this weighing, we determine whether the odd ball is heavy or light

> II. If on this second weighing, the scale tips to Side A, we know that the odd ball is heavy. (If it tips to Side B, we know the odd ball is light, but let's proceed with the assumption that the odd ball is heavy.) We also know that the odd ball is one of the group of three on Side A.

Step 3b: Weigh one of the balls from the group of three against another one. If the scale balances, the ball from the group of three that was unweighed is the odd ball, and is heavy. If the scale tilts, we can identify the odd ball, because we know it is heavier than the other. (If the scale had tipped to Side B, we would use the same logical process, using the knowledge that the odd ball is light.)

Case B: If the balls do not balance on the first weighing

If the balls do not balance on the first weighing, we know that the odd ball is one of the eight balls that was weighed. We also know that the group of four unweighed balls are normal, and that one of the sides, let's say Side A, is heavier than the other (although we don't know whether the odd ball is heavy or light).

Step 2: Take three balls from the unweighed group and use them to replace three balls on Side A (the heavy side). Take the three balls from Side A and use them to replace three balls on Side B (which are removed from the scale).

> I. If the scale balances, we know that one of the balls removed from the scale was the odd one. In this case, we know that the ball is also light. We can proceed with the third weighing as described in step 3b from Case A.

II. If the scale tilts to the other side, so that Side B is now the heavy side, we know that one of the three balls moved from Side A to Side B is the odd ball, and that it is heavy. We proceed with the third weighing as described in step 3b in Case A.

III. If the scale remains the same, we know that one of the two balls on the scale that was not shifted in our second weighing is the odd ball. We also know that the unmoved ball from Side A is heavier than the unmoved ball on Side B (though we don't know whether the odd ball is heavy or light).

Step 3: Weigh the ball from Side A against a normal ball. If the scale balances, the ball from Side B is the odd one, and is light. If the scale does not balance, the ball from Side A is the odd one, and is heavy.

Whew! As you can see from this solution, one of the keys to this problem is understanding that information can be gained about balls even if they are not being weighed. For example, if we know that one of the balls of two groups that are being weighed is the odd ball, we know that the unweighed balls are normal. Once this is known, we realize that breaking the balls up into smaller and smaller groups of three (usually eventually down to three balls), is a good strategy — and an ultimately successful one.

10

You are faced with two doors. One door leads to your job offer (that's the one you want!), and the other leads to the exit. In front of each door is a guard. One guard always tells the truth. The other always lies. You can ask one question to decide which door is the correct one. What will you ask?

The way to logically attack this question is to ask how you can construct a question that provides the same answer (either a true statement or a lie), no matter who you ask.

There are two simple answers. Ask a guard: "If I were to ask you if this door were the correct one, what would you say?" The truthful consultant would answer yes (if it's the correct one), or no (if it's not). Now take the lying consultant. If you asked the liar if the correct door is the right way, he would answer no. But if you ask him: "If I were to ask you if this door were the correct one, what would you say," he would be forced to lie about how he would answer, and say yes. Alternately, ask a guard: "If I were to ask the other guard which way is correct, what would he say?" Here, the truthful guard would tell you the wrong way (because he is truthfully reporting what the liar would say), while the lying guard would also tell you the wrong way (because he is lying about what the truthful guard would say).

If you want to think of this question more mathematically, think of lying as represented by -1, and telling the truth as represented by +1. The first solution provides you with a consistently truthful answer because $(-1)(-1) = 1$, while $(1)(1) = 1$. The second solution provides you with a consistently false answer because $(1)(-1) = -1$, and $(-1)(1) = -1$.

11 **A company has 10 machines that produce gold coins. One of the machines is producing coins that are a gram light. How do you tell which machine is making the defective coins with only one weighing?**

Think this through — clearly, every machine will have to produce a sample coin or coins, and you must weigh all these coins together. How can you somehow indicate which coins came from which machine? The best way to do it is to have every machine crank a different number of coins, so that machine 1 will make one coin, machine 2 will make two coins, and so on. Take all the coins, weigh them together, and consider their weight against the total theoretical weight. If you're four grams short, for example, you'll know that machine 4 is defective.

12 **The four members of U2 (Bono, the Edge, Larry and Adam) need to get across a narrow bridge to play a concert. Since it's dark, a flashlight is required to cross, but the band has only one flashlight, and only two people can cross the bridge at a time. (This is not to say, of course, that if one of the members of the band has crossed the bridge, he can't come back by himself with the flashlight.) Adam takes only a minute to get across, Larry takes two minutes, the Edge takes five minutes, and slowpoke Bono takes 10 minutes. A pair can only go as fast as the slowest member. They have 17 minutes to get across. How should they do it?**

The key to attacking this question is to understand that Bono and the Edge are major liabilities and must be grouped together. In other words, if you sent them across separately, you'd already be using 15 minutes. This won't do.

What does this mean? That Bono and the Edge must go across together. But they can not be the first pair (or one of them will have to transport the flashlight back).

Instead, you send Larry and Adam over first, taking two minutes. Adam comes back, taking another minute, for a total of three minutes. Bono and the Edge then go over, taking 10 minutes, and bringing the total to 13. Larry comes back, taking another two minutes, for a total of 15. Adam and Larry go back over, bringing the total time to 17 minutes.

13. What is the decimal equivalent of ³/16 and ⁷/16?

A commonly-used Wall Street interview question, this one isn't just an attempt to stress you out or see how quick your mind works. This question also has practical banking applications. Stocks often are traded at prices reported in ¹/16s of a dollar. (Each ¹/16 = .0625, so ³/16 = .1875 and ⁷/16 = .4375).

14. What is the sum of the numbers from one to 50?

Another question that recent analyst hires often report receiving. This is a relatively easy one: pair up the numbers into groups of 51 (1 + 50 = 51; 2 + 49 = 51; etc.). Twenty-five pairs of 51 equals 1275.

15. You have a painting that is $320 that is selling for 20 percent off. How much is the discounted price?

Calculate quickly: What's 80 percent of $320? The answer's $256. Even in a question like this, if you are good with numbers and use shortcuts, don't be afraid to talk aloud. For example: 80 percent of $320 can be broken down to a calculation like 80 percent of $80 x $4, or 162.

Vault.com Guide to Finance Interviews
Brainteasers & Guesstimates

16 You're playing three-card monte. Two cards are red, one is black. (Note: In three-card monte, the three cards are face down and you try to pick the black card in order to win.) You pick the middle card. After you pick, the dealer shows that one of the cards you have not chosen is red. You are given the chance to switch your selection. Should you?

The short answer is yes. By switching, you are betting that the card you initially chose was red. By not switching, you are betting that the card you initially chose was black. And because two out of three cards are red, of course, betting on red is the way to go.

Let's break it down, starting with the not switching case. Say the first card you chose was the black one. This happens one-third of the time. If you do not switch your choice, you win. Needless to say, the other two-thirds of the time, having picked a red card, and deciding not to switch, you lose. In other words, if you do not switch, you win a third of the time.

Now let's examine what happens when you switch cards. Say the first card you chose was the black one. Again, this would happen one-third of the time. If, after being shown a red card, you switch, you lose. The other two-thirds of the time, if you switch, you win because the dealer has already shown you that one of the cards you did not pick is red. Given the premise that your original pick was a red card, the card you are switching to must be the black one. You will win two-thirds of the time.

17 A straight flush beats a four-of-a-kind in poker because it is more unlikely. But think about how many straight flushes there are — if you don't count wraparound straights, you can have a straight flush starting on any card from two to 10 in any suit (nine per suit). That means there are 36 straight flushes possible. But how many four of a kinds are there — only 13. What's wrong with this reasoning?

Immediately, you should think about what the difference is between a straight flush and a four-of-a-kind. One involves five cards, and the other involves four. Intuitively, that's what should strike you as the problem with the line of reasoning. Look closer and you'll see what that means: for every four of a kind, there are actually a whole bunch of five-card hands: 48 (52 - 4) in fact. There are actually 624 (48 x 13) of them in all.

18 **If you have seven white socks and nine black socks in a drawer, how many do you have to pull out blindly in order to ensure that you have a matching pair?**

Three. Let's see — if the first one is one color, and the second one is the other color, the third one, no matter what the color, will make a matching pair. Sometimes you're not supposed to think that hard.

19 **Tell me a good joke that is neither sexist nor racist.**

If you can't think of any, you're in the same boat as the unfortunately tongue-tied recent candidate at Salomon Smith Barney. Find one and remember it.

20 **If I were to fill this room with pennies, how many pennies would fit in?**

A literally in-your-face guesstimate.

21 **Say you are driving on a one-mile track. You do one lap at 30 miles an hour. How fast do you have to go to average 60 miles an hour?**

This is something of a trick question, and was recently received by a Goldman candidate. The first thought of many people is to say 90 miles an hour, but consider: If you have done a lap at 30 miles an hour, you have already taken two minutes. Two minutes is the total amount of time you would have to take in order to average 60 miles an hour. Therefore, you can not average 60 miles an hour over the two laps.

Final Analysis

You've probably heard horror stories about finance interviews. Stories about yelling interviewers, rapid-fire math questions, and tough-as-hell finance stumpers. They're not all like that, of course. Plenty of interviews you have as you look for a job in finance will simply be chatty, "tell me about yourself" affairs. But you will get your share of stressful questions. More importantly, when you land that job, you will be asked to perform quick calculations, figure out how a bond or company is priced — and there will be some yelling. If you have read through this guide, you should not only be well prepared for your interviews, but for the position you choose after you ace your interviews. Good luck!

Appendix

Glossary

Accretive merger: A merger in which the acquiring company's earnings per share increase.

Balance Sheet: One of the four basic financial statements, the Balance Sheet presents the financial position of a company at a given point in time, including Assets, Liabilities, and Equity.

Beta: A value that represents the relative volatility of a given investment with respect to the market.

Bond price: The price the bondholder (the lender) pays the bond issuer (the borrower) to hold the bond (i.e. to have a claim on the cash flows documented on the bond).

Bond spreads: The difference between the yield of a corporate bond and a U.S. Treasury security of similar time to maturity.

Buy-side: The clients of investment banks (mutual funds, pension funds) that buy the stocks, bonds and securities sold by the investment banks. (The investment banks that sell these products to investors are known as the "sell-side.")

Callable bond: A bond that can be bought back by the issuer so that it is not committed to paying large coupon payments in the future.

Call option: An option that gives the holder the right to purchase an asset for a specified price on or before a specified expiration date.

Capital Asset Pricing Model (CAPM): A model used to calculate the discount rate of a company's cash flows.

Commercial bank: A bank that lends, rather than raises money. For example, if a company wants $30 million to open a new production plant, it can approach a commercial bank like Chase Manhattan or Citibank for a loan. (Increasingly, commercial banks are also providing investment banking services to clients.)

Commercial paper: Short-term corporate debt, typically maturing in nine months or less.

Commodities: Assets (usually agricultural products or metals) that are generally interchangeable with one another and therefore share a common price. For example, corn, wheat, and rubber generally trade at one price on commodity markets worldwide.

Common stock: Also called common equity, common stock represents an ownership interest in a company. (As opposed to preferred stock, see below.) The vast majority of stock traded in the markets today is common, as common stock enables investors to vote on company matters. An individual with 51 percent or more of shares owned controls a company's decisions and can appoint anyone he/she wishes to the board of directors or to the management team.

Comparable transactions (comps): A method of valuing a company for a merger or acquisition that involves studying similar transactions.

Convertible preferred stock: A relatively uncommon type of equity issued by a company, convertible preferred stock is often issued when it cannot successfully sell either straight common stock or straight debt. Preferred stock pays a dividend, similar to how a bond pays coupon payments, but ultimately converts to common stock after a period of time. It is essentially a mix of debt and equity, and most often used as a means for a risky company to obtain capital when neither debt nor equity works.

Non-convertible preferred stock: Sometimes companies issue non-convertible preferred stock, which remains outstanding in perpetuity and trades like stocks. Utilities represent the best example of non-convertible preferred stock issuers.

Capital market equilibrium: The principle that there should be equilibrium in the global interest rate markets.

Convertible bonds: Bonds that can be converted into a specified number of shares of stock.

Coupon payments: The payments of interest that the bond issuer makes to the bondholder.

Credit ratings: The ratings given to bonds by credit agencies. These ratings indicate the risk of default.

Currency appreciation: When a currency's value is rising relative to other currencies.

Currency depreciation: When a currency's value is falling relative to other currencies.

Currency devaluation: When a currency weakens under fixed exchange rates.

Currency revaluation: When a currency strengthens under fixed exchange rates.

Default premium: The difference between the promised yields on a corporate bond and the yield on an otherwise identical government bond.

Default risk: The risk that the company issuing a bond may go bankrupt and "default" on its loans.

Derivatives: An asset whose value is derived from the price of another asset. Examples include call options, put options, futures, and interest-rate "swaps."

Dilutive merger: A merger in which the acquiring company's earnings per share decrease.

Discount rate: A rate that measures the risk of an investment. It can be understood as the expected return from a project of a certain amount of risk.

Discounted Cash Flow analysis (DCF): A method of valuation that takes the net present value of the free cash flows of a company.

Dividend: A payment by a company to shareholders of its stock, usually as a way to distribute some or all of the profits to shareholders.

Equity: In short, stock. Equity means ownership in a company that is usually represented by stock.

The Fed: The Federal Reserve, which gently (or sometimes roughly), manages the country's economy by setting interest rates.

Fixed income: Bonds and other securities that earn a fixed rate of return. Bonds are typically issued by governments, corporations and municipalities.

Float: The number of shares available for trade in the market times the price. Generally speaking, the bigger the float, the greater the stock's liquidity.

Floating rate: An interest rate that is benchmarked to other rates (such as the rate paid on U.S. Treasuries), allowing the interest rate to change as market conditions change.

Forward contract: A contract that calls for future delivery of an asset at an agreed-upon price.

Forward exchange rate: The price of currencies at which they can be bought and sold for future delivery.

Forward rates (for bonds): The agreed-upon interst rates for a bond to be issued in the future.

Futures contract: A contract that calls for the delivery of an asset or its cash value at a specified delivery or maturity date for an agreed upon price. A future is a type of forward contract that is liquid, standardized, traded on an exchange, and whose prices are settled at the end of each trading day.

Glass-Steagall Act: Part of the legislation passed during the Depression (Glass-Steagall was passed in 1933) designed to help prevent future bank failure — the establishment of the F.D.I.C. was also part of this movement. The Glass-Steagall Act split America's investment banking (issuing and trading securities) operations from commercial banking (lending). For example, J.P. Morgan was forced to spin off its securities unit as Morgan Stanley. Since the late 1980s, the Federal Reserve has steadily weakened the act, allowing commercial banks such as NationsBank and Bank of America to buy investment banks like Montgomery Securities and Robertson Stephens.

Goodwill: An account that includes intangible assets a company may have, such as brand image.

Hedge: To balance a position in the market in order to reduce risk. Hedges work like insurance: a small position pays off large amounts with a slight move in the market.

High yield bonds (a.k.a. junk bonds): Bonds with poor credit ratings that pay a relatively high rate of interest.

Holding Period Return: The income earned over a period as a percentage of the bond price at the start of the period.

Income Statement: One of the four basic financial statements, the Income Statement presents the results of operations of a business over a specified period of time, and is composed of Revenues, Expenses, and Net Income.

Initial Public Offering (IPO): The dream of every entrepreneur, the IPO is the first time a company issues stock to the public. "Going public" means more than raising money for the company: By agreeing to take on public shareholders, a company enters a whole world of required SEC filings and quarterly revenue and earnings reports, not to mention possible shareholder lawsuits.

Investment grade bonds: Bonds with high credit ratings that pay a relatively low rate of interest.

Leveraged Buyout (LBO): The buyout of a company with borrowed money, often using that company's own assets as collateral. LBOs were the order of the day in the heady 1980s, when successful LBO firms such as Kohlberg Kravis Roberts made a practice of buying up companies, restructuring them, and reselling them or taking them public at a significant profit. LBOs are now somewhat out of fashion.

Liquidity: The amount of a particular stock or bond available for trading in the market. For commonly traded securities, such as big cap stocks and U.S. government bonds, they are said to be highly liquid instruments. Small cap stocks and smaller fixed income issues often are called illiquid (as they are not actively traded) and suffer a liquidity discount, i.e. they trade at lower valuations to similar, but more liquid, securities.

The Long Bond: The 30-year U.S. Treasury bond. Treasury bonds are used as the starting point for pricing many other bonds, because Treasury bonds are assumed to have zero credit risk take into account factors such as inflation. For example, a company will issue a bond that trades "40 over Treasuries." The 40 refers to 40 basis points (100 basis points = 1 percentage point).

Market Cap(italization): The total value of a company in the stock market (total shares outstanding x price per share).

Money market securities: This term is generally used to represent the market for securities maturing within one year. These include short-term CDs, Repurchase Agreements, Commercial Paper (low-risk corporate issues), among others. These are low risk, short-term securities that have yields similar to Treasuries.

Mortgage-backed bonds: Bonds collateralized by a pool of mortgages. Interest and principal payments are based on the individual homeowners making their mortgage payments. The more diverse the pool of mortgages backing the bond, the less risky they are.

Multiples method: A method of valuing a company that involves taking a multiple of an indicator such as price-to-earnings, EBITDA, or revenues.

Municipal bonds: Bonds issued by local and state governments, a.k.a. municipalities. Municipal bonds are structured as tax-free for the investor, which means investors in "muni's" earn interest payments without having to pay federal taxes. Sometimes investors are exempt from state and local taxes, too. Consequently, municipalities can pay lower interest rates on muni bonds than other bonds of similar risk.

Net present value (NPV): The present value of a series of cash flows generated by an investment, minus the initial investment. NPV is calculated because of the important concept that "money today is worth more than the same money tomorrow."

Par value: The total amount a bond issuer will commit to pay back when the bond expires.

P/E ratio: The price to earnings ratio. This is the ratio of a company's stock price to its earnings-per-share. The higher the P/E ratio, the more "expensive" a stock is (and also the faster investors believe the company will grow). Stocks in fast-growing industries tend to have higher P/E ratios.

Pooling accounting: A type of accounting used in a stock swap merger. Pooling accounting does not account for Goodwill, and is preferable to purchase accounting.

Prime rate: The average rate U.S. banks charge to companies for loans.

Purchase accounting: A type of accounting used in a merger with a considerable amount of cash. Purchase accounting takes Goodwill into account, and is less preferable than pooling accounting.

Put option: An option that gives the holder the right to sell an asset for a specified price on or before a specified expiration date.

Securities and Exchange Commission (SEC): A federal agency that, like the Glass-Steagall Act, was established as a result of the stock market crash of 1929 and the ensuing depression. The SEC monitors disclosure of financial information to stockholders, and protects against fraud. Publicly traded securities must first be approved by the SEC prior to trading.

Securitize: To convert an asset into a security that can then be sold to investors. Nearly any income-generating asset can be turned into a security. For example, a 20-year mortgage on a home can be packaged with other mortgages just like it, and shares in this pool of mortgages can then be sold to investors.

Spot exchange rate: The price of currencies for immediate delivery.

Statement of Cash Flows: One of the four basic financial statements, the Statement of Cash Flows presents a detailed summary of all of the cash inflows and outflows during a specified period.

Statement of Retained Earnings: One of the four basic financial statements, the Statement of Retained Earnings is a reconciliation of the Retained Earnings account. Information such as dividends or announced income is provided in the statement. The Statement of Retained Earnings provides information about what a company's management is doing with the company's earnings.

Stock: Ownership in a company.

Stock swap: A form of M&A activity in whereby the stock of one company is exchanged for the stock of another.

Strong currency: A currency whose value is rising relative to other currencies.

Swap: A type of derivative, a swap is an exchange of future cash flows. Popular swaps include foreign exchange swaps and interest rate swaps.

10K: An annual report filed by a public company with the Securities and Exchange Commission (SEC). Includes financial information, company information, risk factors, etc.

Tender offers: A method by which a hostile acquirer renders an offer to the shareholders of a company in an attempt to gather a controlling interest in the company. Generally, the potential acquirer will offer to buy stock from shareholders at a much higher value than the market value.

Treasury securities: Securities issued by the U.S. government. These are divided into Treasury bills (maturity of up to 2 years), Treasury notes (from 2 years to 10 years maturity), and Treasury bonds (10 years to 30 years). As they are government guaranteed, often treasuries are considered "risk-free." In fact, while U.S. Treasuries have no default risk, they do have interest rate risk; if rates increase, then the price of UST's will decrease.

Underwrite: The function performed by investment banks when they help companies issue securities to investors. Technically, the investment bank buys the securities from the company and immediately resells the securities to investors for a slightly higher price, making money on the spread.

Weak currency: A currency whose value is falling relative to other currencies.

Yield to call: The yield of a bond calculated up to the period when the bond is called (paid off by the bond issuer).

Yield: The annual return on investment. A high-yield bond, for example, pays a high rate of interest.

Yield to maturity: The measure of the average rate of return that will be earned on a bond if it is bought now and held to maturity.

Zero coupon bonds: A bond that offers no coupon or interest payments to the bondholder.

About the Author

D. Bhatawedekhar is the pen name of an associate with one of Wall Street's bulge bracket investment banking firms. He is a graduate of the University of Chicago's Graduate School of Business, and majored in finance.

Vault.com Career Industry Guides

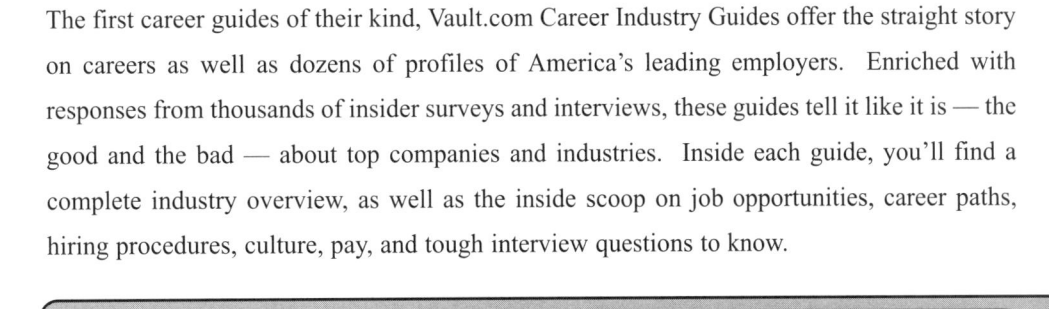

The first career guides of their kind, Vault.com Career Industry Guides offer the straight story on careers as well as dozens of profiles of America's leading employers. Enriched with responses from thousands of insider surveys and interviews, these guides tell it like it is — the good and the bad — about top companies and industries. Inside each guide, you'll find a complete industry overview, as well as the inside scoop on job opportunities, career paths, hiring procedures, culture, pay, and tough interview questions to know.

The Vault.com Guide to America's Top 50 Law Firms, *2nd edition*
768 pages

The Vault.com Career Guide to Investment Banking
384 pages

The Vault.com Career Guide to Consulting
320 pages

The Vault.com Career Guide to Marketing & Brand Management
375 pages

The Vault.com Career Guide to Media and Entertainment
452 pages

The Vault.com Career Guide to the High Tech Industry
458 pages

The Vault.com Guide to the Top 50 MBA Employers
501 pages

The Vault.com Career Guide to Accounting
250 pages

The Vault.com Career Guide to the Fashion Industry
250 pages

The Vault.com Career Guide to Advertising & Public Relations
250 pages

VAULT.COM

$35 PER PRINTED VERSION OF GUIDE, OR VIEW FOR FREE ONLINE

To order call 1.888.562.8285 or order online at www.Vault.com

Get the Inside Scoop on Investment Banking

The Vault.com Career Guide to Investment Banking

Are you interested in a position in investment banking? Then this book is your entrée into the fast-paced and lucrative investment banking industry. The guide includes a detailed look at the roles and lifestyles of investment banking professionals, from the all-nighters of the financial-model building corporate finance analyst to the pressure-packed position as an influential stock research analyst, to the schmoozing of the private client sales associate.

Plus, Vault.com has interviewed and surveyed hundreds of banking insiders to bring you the inside scoop on more than 30 leading I-banks. Our insiders give you the real scoop on pay, corporate culture, travel and other vital information that every prospective investment banker needs to know. This guide contains the most up-to-date, accurate information on investment banks available.

Just how many hours will you really work a week? What kind of clients does each investment bank serve? What do you need to do to get the most desirable investment banking positions? You'll find the answers — and much more — in the Vault.com Career Guide to Investment Banking.

384 pages • $35

VAULT.COM

Get the Straight Story on Investment Banking...

- How much can you expect to make as an analyst or associate at Wall Street and regional firms?
- What bankers do on "roadshows" leading up to public offerings?
- Why should you look very carefully at you research analyst before signing on as a research associate?
- At which firm analysts play basketball with partners and boogie-down on the dance floor with the CEO?
- At which firm bankers wear shorts and don't work on the weekends?

To order call (888) 562-8285 or order online at www.Vault.com

VAULT JOB BOARD

A Free Online Service for Job Seekers!

With tens of thousands of postings from over 6,000 employers (and counting!) the Vault Job Board has the jobs you want. We receive thousands of great jobs for lawyers and experienced professionals weekly!

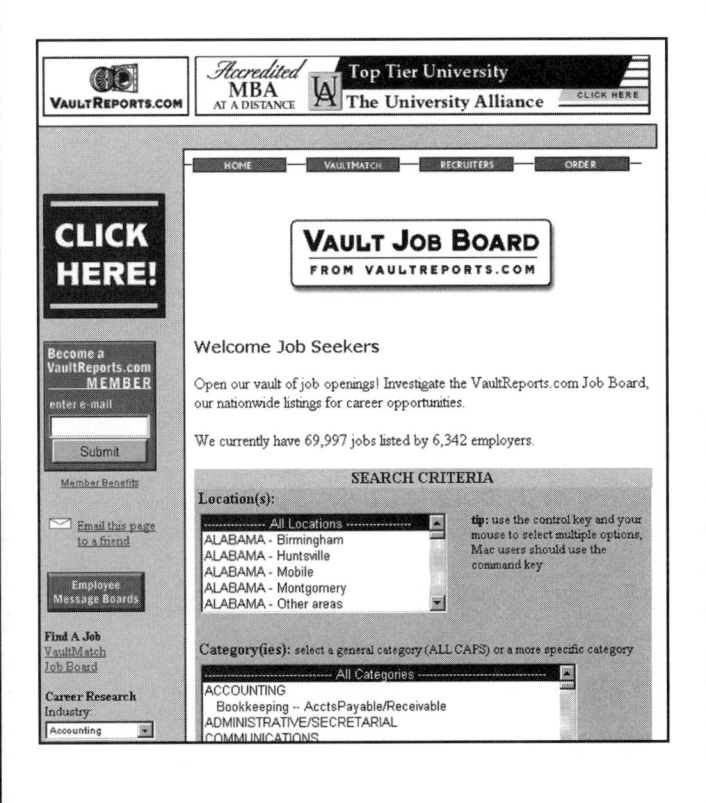

Some of our top-notch employers include:

3Com
About.com
AT&T
Barnes and Noble
Bloomberg
CMP Media
Deja.com
Deloitte & Touche
Donaldson, Lufkin & Jenrette
HBO
Hewlett Packard
Intel
iVillage
KPMG
Lehman Brothers
Microsoft
Morgan Stanley Dean Witter
Oracle Corporation
PriceWaterhouseCoopers

And many more!

Would you like to submit a job to the Vault Job Board?
Click on www.Vault.com or e-mail marketing@vault.com

JOB SEEKERS:

Have job openings that match your criteria e-mailed to you for free!

VAULTMATCH™
FROM VAULT.COM

VAULT.COM — THE WORKPLACE NETWORK

A free service for job seekers!

Vault.com will e-mail job postings to you which match your interests and qualifications. It's free, it's easy and it's effective! Here's how it works:

1. You visit www.Vault.com and fill out an online questionnaire, indicating your qualifications and the types of positions you want.
2. Companies contact VaultReports.com with job openings.
3. VaultReports.com sends you an e-mail about each position which matches your qualifications and interests.
4. For each position that interests you, simply reply to the e-mail and attach your resume. You make the decision to respond – so VaultMatch is always confidential
5. VaultMatch is always free to you. Sign up today!

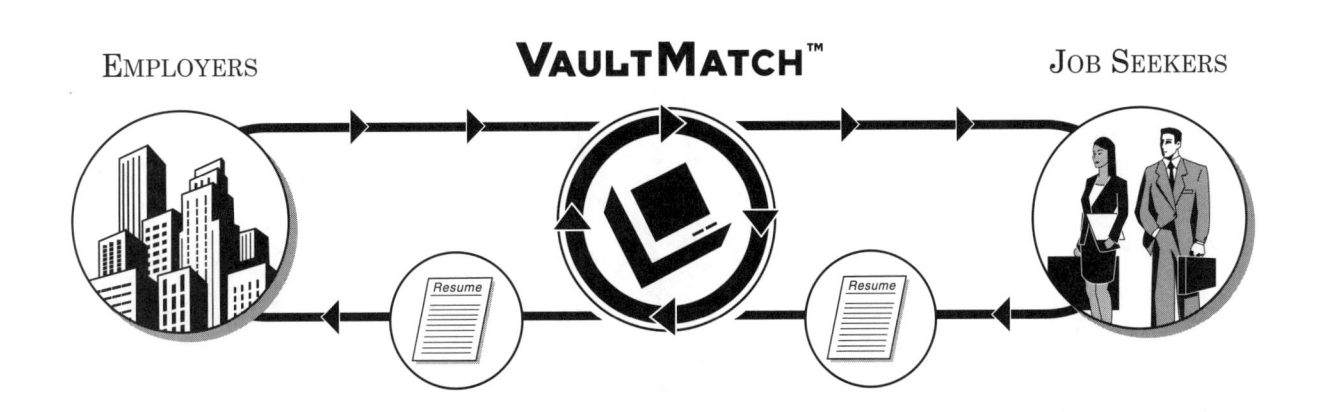

EMPLOYERS   **VAULTMATCH**™   JOB SEEKERS

EMPLOYERS: Put VaultMatch to work for you. Register at www.Vault.com

www.Vault.com

In the 1980s, Greed was Good.
In the Information Age...
GOSSIP IS GOOD

VAULT.COM™
MESSAGE BOARDS

Use our Message Boards to:

- Share in the latest company gossip
- Get the inside scoop on pay, perks and bonuses
- Hear about interviews from recent candidates
- Mix and interact with other job seekers
- Post messages and start your own discussions

Come see what they are saying now about the employers on your interview list!

Message boards available on 1000s of top employers, including:

3Com	Cargill	The Gap	Morgan Stanley
A.T. Kearney	Citibank/Citigroup	General Mills	Netscape Comunications
Abbott Laboratories	Clorox	Goldman, Sachs & Co	Nike
America Online	Coca-Cola	Hewlett-Packard	Oracle
American Express	Colgate-Palmolive	IBM	Procter & Gamble
AMS	Credit Suisse First Boston	Intel	PricewaterhouseCoopers
Andersen Consulting	Dell Computer	Johnson & Johnson	Salomon Smith Barney
Arthur D. Little	Deloitte Consulting	J.P. Morgan	Silicon Graphics
Aveda	DLJ	KPMG Consulting	Sprint
Bain	Enron	Levi Strauss	Sun Microsystems
Bankers Trust	Ernst & Young	Merck	Time Warner
Boston Consulting Group	Fidelity	Microsoft	Walt Disney
Booz-Allen & Hamilton	Ford Motor Company	Mobil	

W W W . V A U L T . C O M

Corporate Recruiters

Strengthen your recruiting efforts with

VAULT.COM

Online Sponsorship Opportunies

- Your company has the opportunity to place a banner on a particular set of Company pages, including your own page and your competitors' pages.
- Your company may place a banner on a particular Industry and Career page.
- Sponsorship of the Company and Industry page is a highly effective way to reach your target demographic.

Snapshot & Highlights Page

- Your on-line Snapshot is an in-depth analysis of your company by VaultReports.com.
- The Highlights page is a compilation of the most positive attributes from the report on your company.
- The Highlights page will appear on our web-site and can be linked directly to your site and also reprinted for off-line recruiting and promotional use.

Online Company Q&A

- We can customize an on-line Q&A which serves as a 1st party endorsement.
- Your Q&A gives you the opportunity to discuss corporate programs, policies, initiatives and strategies in an in-depth manner.
- Your Q&A can also be linked directly from our site to yours. ($795/month)

For more info call Vault.com Corporate Sales (212) 366-4212 or e-mail sales@vault.com